# Standards Practice

## For Home or School

### Grade K

**INCLUDES:**

- Home or School Practice
- Lesson Practice and Test Preparation
- English and Spanish School-Home Letters
- Getting Ready for Grade 1 Lessons

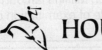 HOUGHTON MIFFLIN HARCOURT

Printed in the U.S.A.

ISBN 978-0-547-58812-4

14 15  1421  20 19 18 17 16 15 14

4500463642        C D E F G

 **Number and Operations**

 **Critical Area** Representing, relating, and operating on whole numbers, initially with sets of objects

# 1 Represent, Count, and Write Numbers 0 to 5

**Domains** Counting and Cardinality
Operations and Algebraic Thinking
**Common Core Standards** CC.K.CC.3, CC.K.CC.4a, CC.K.CC.4b, CC.K.OA.3

# 2 Compare Numbers to 5

**Domain** Counting and Cardinality
**Common Core Standards** CC.K.CC.6

**iii**

## 3 Represent, Count, and Write Numbers 6 to 9

**Domains** Counting and Cardinality
**Common Core Standards** CC.K.CC.3, CC.K.CC.5, CC.K.CC.6

## 4 Represent and Compare Numbers to 10

**Domain** Counting and Cardinality
Operations and Algebraic Thinking
**Common Core Standards** CC.K.CC.2, CC.K.CC.3, CC.K.CC.5, CC.K.CC.6, CC.K.CC.7, CC.K.OA.4

## 5 Addition

**Domains** Operations and Algebraic Thinking
**Common Core Standards** CC.K.OA.1, CC.K.OA.2, CC.K.OA.3, CC.K.OA.4, CC.K.OA.5

## 6 Subtraction

**Domains** Operations and Algebraic Thinking
**Common Core Standards** CC.K.OA.1, CC.K.OA.2, CC.K.OA.5

# 7 Represent, Count, and Write 11 to 19

**Domains** Counting and Cardinality
Number and Operations in Base Ten
**Common Core Standards** CC.K.CC.3, CC.K.NBT.1

© Houghton Mifflin Harcourt Publishing Company

# CRITICAL AREA  Geometry and Positions

**COMMON CORE**  **Critical Area** Describing shapes and space

© Houghton Mifflin Harcourt Publishing Company

# 10 Identify and Describe Three-Dimensional Shapes

**Domain** Geometry

**Common Core Standards** CC.K.G.1, CC.K.G.2, CC.K.G.3, CC.K.G.4

# CRITICAL AREA  Measurement and Data

**COMMON CORE**  **Critical Area** Representing, relating, and operating on whole numbers, initially with sets of objects

## 11  Measurement

**Domains** Measurement and Data
**Common Core Standards** CC.K.MD.1, CC.K.MD.2

## 12  Classify and Sort Data

**Domains** Measurement and Data
**Common Core Standards** CC.K.MD.3

# End-of-Year Resources

## Getting Ready for Grade 1

These lessons review important skills and prepare you for Grade 1.

# School-Home
# Letter

## Dear Family,

My class started Chapter 1 this week. In this chapter, I will show, count, and write numbers 0 to 5.

Love, _____

## Vocabulary

**one** a number for a single object

**two** one more than one

## Home Activity

Use this five frame and counters, such as buttons. Have your child place counters in the five frame to show the numbers 0 to 5. For 0, have your child place one counter in the five frame, and then remove it. Together, practice writing the numbers 0 to 5.

## Literature

Look for this book in a library. This book will reinforce your child's counting skills.

**Fish Eyes: A Book You Can Count On** by Lois Ehlert. Voyager Books, 1992.

# Carta
## para la casa

## Querida familia:

Mi clase comenzó el Capítulo 1 esta semana. En este capítulo mostraré, contaré y escribiré números del 0 al 5.

Con cariño, _____

## Vocabulario

**uno** el número de un solo objeto

**dos** uno más que uno

## Actividad para la casa

Use este cuadro de cinco y fichas, tales como botones. Pídale a su hijo que ponga las fichas en el cuadro para mostrar los números del 0 al 5. Para 0, pídale que coloque una ficha en el cuadro de cinco y luego que la quite. Juntos, practiquen la escritura de los números del 0 al 5.

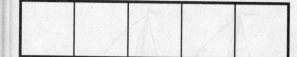

## Literatura

Busque este libro en una biblioteca. Este libro ayudarán a su hijo a reforzar la destreza de contar.

**Fish Eyes: A Book You Can Count On**
por Lois Ehlert.
Voyager Books, 1992.

Name _____

# Model and Count 1 and 2

**COMMON CORE STANDARD** CC.K.CC.4a
Count to tell the number of objects.

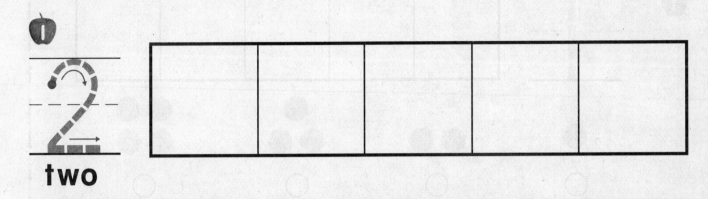

two

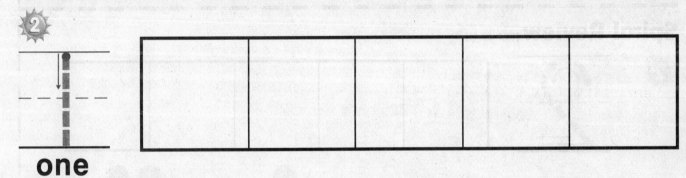

one

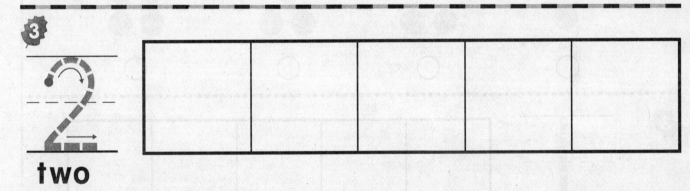

two

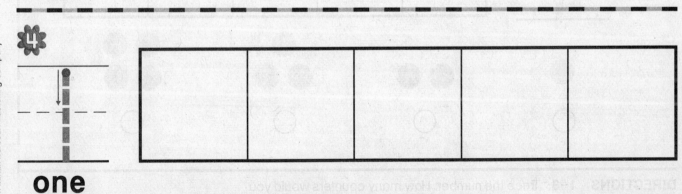

one

**DIRECTIONS** 1–4. Say the number. Count out that many counters in the five frame. Draw the counters.

## Lesson Check (CC.K.CC.4a)

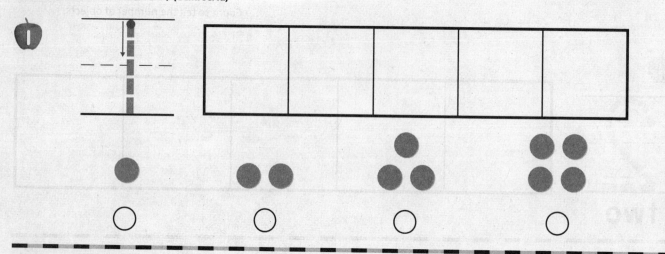

## Spiral Review (CC.K.CC.4a)

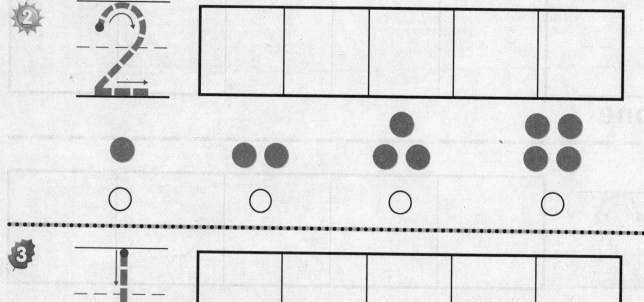

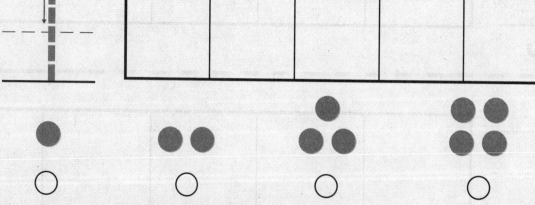

**DIRECTIONS  1–3.** Trace the number. How many counters would you place in the five frame to show the number? Mark under your answer. (Lesson 1.1)

Name _____

# Count and Write 1 and 2

COMMON CORE STANDARD CC.K.CC.3
Know number names and the
count sequence.

**DIRECTIONS** 1–4. Count and tell how many. Write the number.

**Chapter 1**

# Lesson Check (CC.K.CC.3)

| 1 | 2 | 3 | 4 |

○   ○   ○   ○

# Spiral Review (CC.K.CC.4a)

  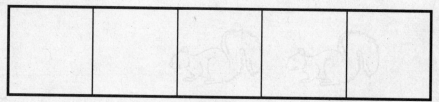

 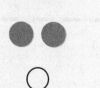  

○   ○   ○   ○

 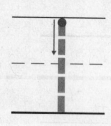 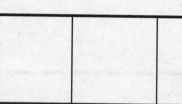 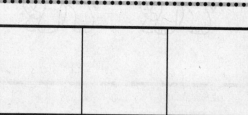

**DIRECTIONS** 1. Count and tell how many cubes. Mark under your answer. (Lesson 1.2)  2-3. Trace the number. How many counters would you place in the five frame to show the number? Mark under your answer. (Lesson 1.1)

Name _____

# Model and Count 3 and 4

**COMMON CORE STANDARD** CC.K.CC.4a
Count to tell the number of objects.

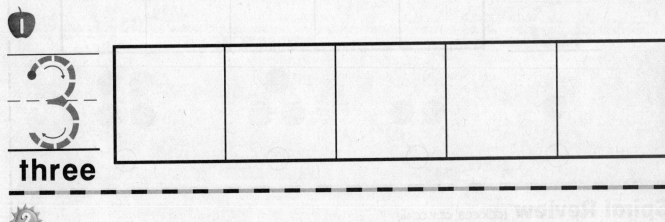

**①**

3

**three**

**②**

4

**four**

**③**

3

**three**

**④**

4

**four**

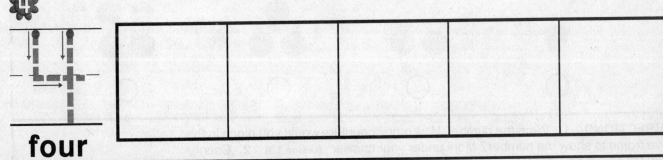

**DIRECTIONS** 1–4. Say the number as you trace it. Count out that many counters in the five frame. Draw the counters.

# Lesson Check (CC.K.CC.4a)

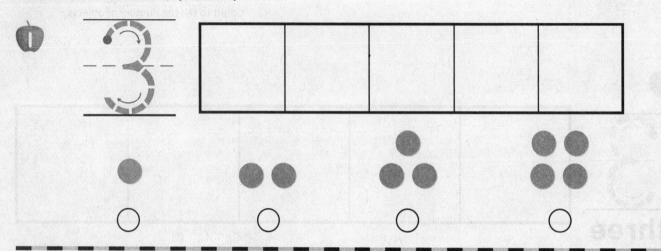

# Spiral Review (CC.K.CC.3, CC.K.CC.4a)

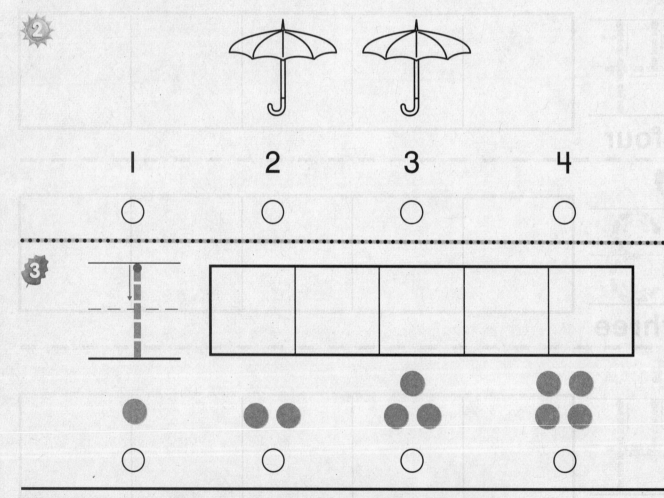

**DIRECTIONS** **1.** Trace the number. How many counters would you place in the five frame to show the number? Mark under your answer. **(Lesson 1.3)** **2.** Count and tell how many umbrellas. Mark under your answer. **(Lesson 1.2)** **3.** Trace the number. How many counters would you place in the five frame to show the number? Mark under your answer. **(Lesson 1.1)**

Name _____

# Count and Write 3 and 4

COMMON CORE STANDARD CC.K.CC.3
Know number names and the count sequence.

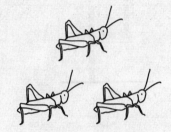

3

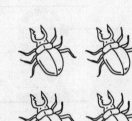

_____

- - - - - - - - - - - - - -

_____

---

3

_____

- - - - - - - - - - - - - -

_____

4

_____

- - - - - - - - - - - - - -

_____

---

5

_____

- - - - - - - - - - - - - -

_____

6

_____

- - - - - - - - - - - - - -

_____

**DIRECTIONS**  1–6. Count and tell how many. Write the number.

# Lesson Check (CC.K.CC.3)

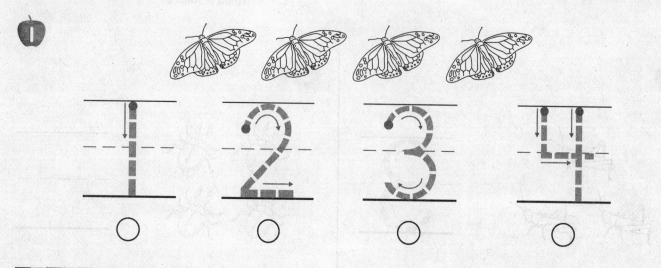

# Spiral Review (CC.K.CC.3, CC.K.CC.4a)

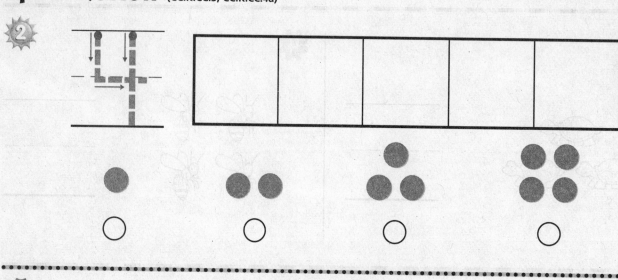

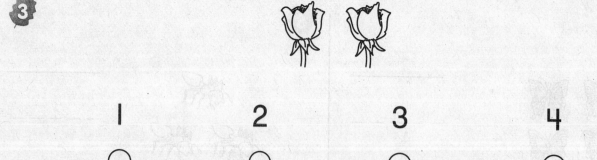

| 1 | 2 | 3 | 4 |
| :-: | :-: | :-: | :-: |
| ○ | ○ | ○ | ○ |

**DIRECTIONS** **1.** Count and tell how many butterflies. Mark under your answer. **(Lesson 1.4)** **2.** Trace the number. How many counters would you place in the five frame to show the number? Mark under your answer. **(Lesson 1.3)** **3.** Count and tell how many flowers. Mark under your answer. **(Lesson 1.2)**

**HANDS ON**
**Lesson 1.5**

Name _____

# Model and Count 5

**COMMON CORE STANDARD** CC.K.CC.4a
Count to tell the number of objects.

**1**

| | | | | |
|---|---|---|---|---|
| | | | | |

_____
- - - - - -
_____

**2**

| | | | | |
|---|---|---|---|---|
| | | | | |

_____

_____

**3**

| | | | | |
|---|---|---|---|---|
| | | | | |

_____
- - - - - -

**4**

| | | | | |
|---|---|---|---|---|
| | | | | |

_____
- - - - - -
_____

**DIRECTIONS** **1.** Place counters to show five. Draw the counters. Write the number. **2.** Place counters to show three. Draw the counters. Write the number. **3.** Place counters to show four. Draw the counters. Write the number. **4.** Place counters to show five. Draw the counters. Write the number.

# Lesson Check (CC.K.CC.4a)

 **1**

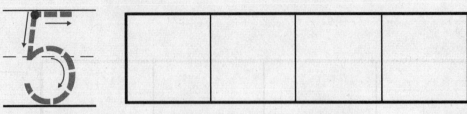

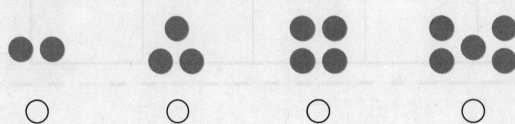

○   ○   ○   ○

# Spiral Review (CC.K.CC.3)

 **2**

1    2    3    4

○   ○   ○   ○

 **3**

1    2    3    4

○   ○   ○   ○

**DIRECTIONS** 1. Trace the number. How many counters would you place in the five frame to show the number? Mark under your answer.
(Lesson 1.5) 2. Count and tell how many cars. Mark under your answer.
(Lesson 1.4) 3. Count and tell how many fish. Mark under your answer.
(Lesson 1.2)

# Count and Write 5

COMMON CORE STANDARDS CC.K.CC.4b
Count to tell the number of objects.

**1**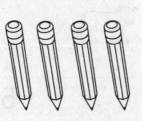

_ _ _ _ _ _ _ _

_____

**2**

_ _ _ _ _ _ _ _

_____

**3**

_____

_ _ _ _ _ _ _ _

_____

**4**

_____

_ _ _ _ _ _ _ _

_____

**5**

_ _ _ _ _ _ _ _

_____

**6**

_____

_ _ _ _ _ _ _ _

_____

**DIRECTIONS** 1–6. Count and tell how many. Write the number.

## Lesson Check (CC.K.CC.4b)

| 2 | 3 | 4 | 5 |
|---|---|---|---|
| ○ | ○ | ○ | ○ |

## Spiral Review (CC.K.CC.3, CC.K.CC.4a)

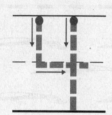 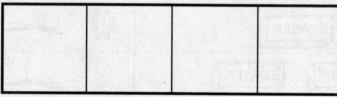

| 2 | 3 | 4 | 5 |
|---|---|---|---|
| ○ | ○ | ○ | ○ |

**DIRECTIONS** **I.** Count and tell how many animals. Mark under your answer.
**(Lesson 1.6)** **2.** Trace the number. How many counters would you place in the
five frame to show the number? Mark under your answer. **(Lesson 1.3)** **3.** Count
and tell how many pieces of pepperoni. Mark under your answer. **(Lesson 1.2)**

Name _____

# Algebra • Ways to Make 5

COMMON CORE STANDARD CC.K.OA.3
Understand addition as putting together and
adding to, and understand subtraction as
taking apart and taking from.

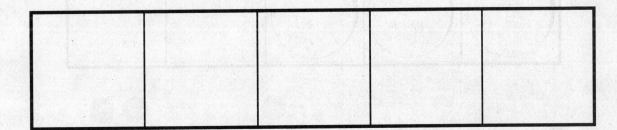

 **and**

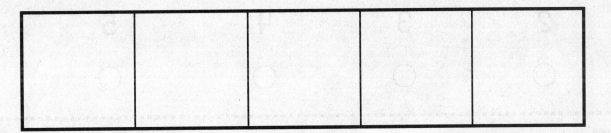

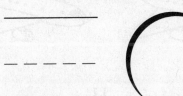 **and**

**DIRECTIONS** 1–2. Use two colors of counters to show a way to
make 5. Color to show the counters. Write the numbers to show the
pair that makes 5.

# Lesson Check (CC.K.OA.3)

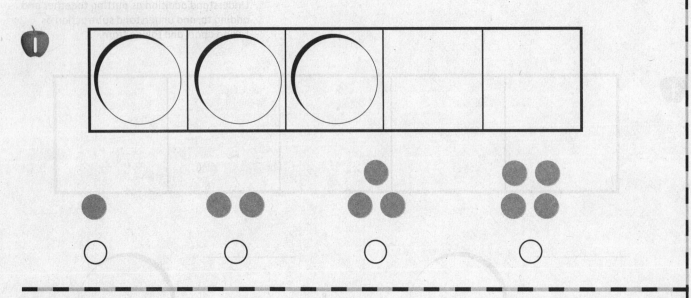

# Spiral Review (CC.K.CC.3, CC.K.CC.4b)

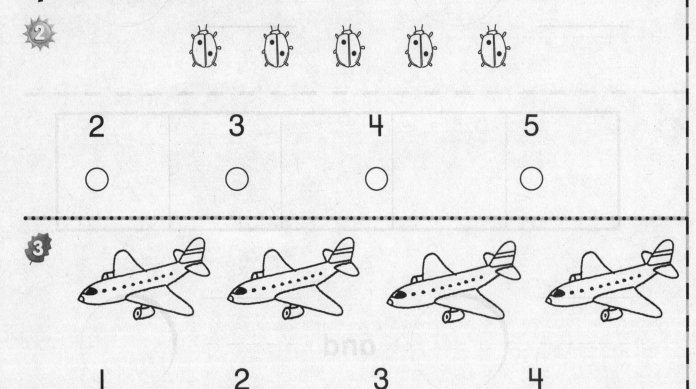

**DIRECTIONS 1.** How many more counters would you place in the five frame to show a way to make 5? Mark under your answer. **(Lesson 1.7) 2.** Count and tell how many ladybugs. Mark under your answer. **(Lesson 1.6) 3.** Count and tell how many airplanes. Mark under your answer. **(Lesson 1.4)**

**P16** sixteen

# Count and Order to 5

COMMON CORE STANDARD CC.K.CC.4c
Count to tell the number of objects.

**1**

**DIRECTIONS**   I. Count the objects in each set. Write the number beside the set of objects. Write those numbers in order beginning with number I.

## Lesson Check (CC.K.CC.4c)

1, 2, 3, 4, 5 | 2, 1, 3, 4, 5 | 3, 2, 1, 4, 5 | 5, 4, 1, 2, 3

○　　　　　○　　　　　○　　　　　○

## Spiral Review (CC.K.CC.3c, CC.K.CC.4a)

2　　　　　3　　　　　4　　　　　5

○　　　　　○　　　　　○　　　　　○

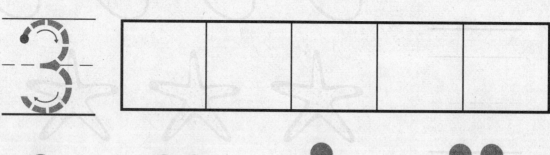

○　　　　　○　　　　　○　　　　　○

**DIRECTIONS** 1. Which set of numbers is in order? Mark under your answer. (Lesson 1.8) 2. Count and tell how many stars. Mark under your answer. (Lesson 1.4) 3. Trace the number. How many counters would you place in the five frame to show the number? Mark under your answer. (Lesson 1.3)

# Problem Solving • Understand 0

**COMMON CORE STANDARD** CC.K.CC.3
Know number names and the
count sequence.

**1**

_____

– – – – – –

_____

- - - - - - - - - - - - - - - - - - - - - - - - - - - - - - - - -

**2**

_____

– – – – – 0

_____

**DIRECTIONS** Use counters to model these problems.  **1.** Oliver has one juice box. Lucy has one fewer juice box than Oliver. How many juice boxes does Lucy have? Write the number.  **2.** Jessica has no books. Wesley has 2 more books than Jessica. How many books does Wesley have? Write the number.

© Houghton Mifflin Harcourt Publishing Company

# Lesson Check (CC.K.CC.3)

| 0 | 1 | 2 | 3 |
|---|---|---|---|
| ○ | ○ | ○ | ○ |

# Spiral Review (CC.K.CC.3)

| 2 | 3 | 4 | 5 |
|---|---|---|---|
| ○ | ○ | ○ | ○ |

| 0 | 1 | 2 | 3 |
|---|---|---|---|
| ○ | ○ | ○ | ○ |

**DIRECTIONS** 1. Eva has 2 apples in her basket. She eats 1 apple and gives 1 apple to her friend. How many apples does Eva have now? Mark under your answer. **(Lesson 1.9)**
2. Count and tell how many cubes. Mark under your answer. **(Lesson 1.4)**
3. Count and tell how many squirrels. Mark under your answer. **(Lesson 1.2)**

# Identify and Write 0

COMMON CORE STANDARDS CC.K.CC.3
Know number names and the
count sequence.

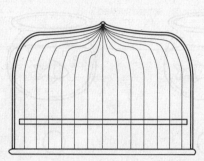

_____

_ _ _ _ _ _ _ _

_____

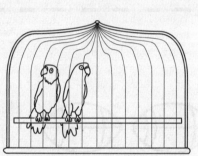

_____

_ _ _ _ _ _ _ _

_____

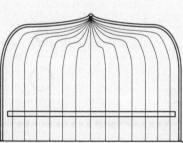

_____

_ _ _ _ _ _ _ _

_____

_____

_ _ _ _ _ _ _ _

_____

**DIRECTIONS** I–4. How many birds are in the cage? Write the
number. Circle the cages that have 0 birds.

# Lesson Check (CC.K.CC.3)

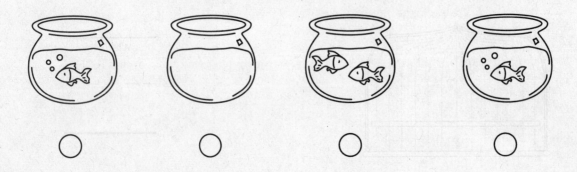

◯    ◯    ◯    ◯

# Spiral Review (CC.K.CC.4a, CC.K.CC.4b)

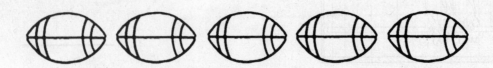

**2**    **3**    **4**    **5**

◯    ◯    ◯    ◯

◯    ◯    ◯    ◯

**DIRECTIONS** 1. Which bowl has 0 fish? Mark under your answer. (Lesson 1.10) 2. Count and tell how many footballs. Mark under your answer. (Lesson 1.6) 3. Which group shows 5 objects? Mark under your answer. (Lesson 1.5)

COMMON CORE STANDARDS CC.K.CC.3, CC.K.CC.4a, CC.K.CC.4b, CC. K.CC.4c

# Chapter 1 Extra Practice

## Lessons 1.1 – 1.6 (pp. 13 – 36) • • • • • • • • • • • • • • • • • • • • • • • • • • •

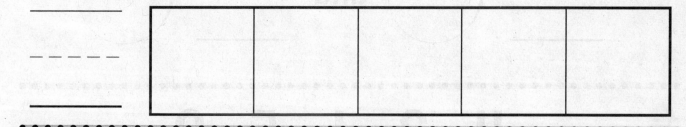

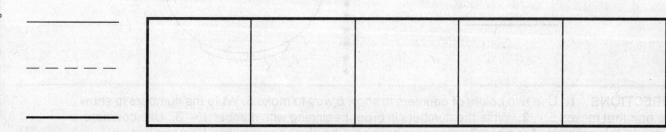

**DIRECTIONS** 1–3. Place a counter on each object in the set as you count them. Tell how many counters. Write the number. Move the counters to the five frame. Draw the counters.

**1**

| | | | | |
|---|---|---|---|---|

_____  ◯  **and**  _____  ◯

_____

**2**

# 4, 3, 1, 5, 2

**3**                    **4**

**DIRECTIONS    1.** Use two colors of counters to show a way to make 5. Write the numbers to show the pair that makes 5.    **2.** Write the numbers in order beginning with number 1.    **3.** Use counters to model this problem. Anna has 2 oranges in her bag. She gives some away. Now she has no oranges. How many oranges did she give away? Write the number.    **4.** Write the number to show how many fish are in the bowl.

# School-Home Letter

## Dear Family,

My class started Chapter 2 this week. In this chapter, I will learn how to build and compare sets to help me compare numbers.

Love, _____

## Vocabulary

**same number**

 There are the same number of circles and triangles.

**greater**

The number of circles is greater than the number of triangles.

**less**

The number of circles is less than the number of triangles.

## Home Activity

Gather two sets of five household items. Line some of them up on a table in two groups of different quantities. Ask your child to count and tell you how many are in each set. Have your child point to the set that has the greater number of objects. Then ask your child to point to the set with the number of objects that is less.

Change the number in each group and repeat the activity.

## Literature

Look for this book in the library. It will help reinforce concepts of comparing.

**More, Fewer, Less** by Tana Hoban. Greenwillow Books, 1998.

# Carta
## para la casa

## Querida familia:

Mi clase comenzó el Capítulo 2 esta semana. En este capítulo, aprenderé cómo construir y comparar conjuntos que me ayuden a comparar números.

Con cariño, _____

## Vocabulario

**igual número**

Hay igual número de círculos y triángulos.

**mayor**

El número de círculos es mayor que el número de triángulos.

**menor**

El número de círculos es menor que el número de triángulos.

## Actividad para la casa

Reúna dos conjuntos con cinco elementos de la casa. Alinee sobre la mesa algunos de ellos en dos grupos de diferentes cantidades. Pídale a su hijo que cuente y diga cuántos hay en cada conjunto. Dígale que señale el conjunto que tiene el mayor número de objetos. Luego, pídale que señale el conjunto con el menor número de objetos.

Cambie el número en cada grupo y repita la actividad.

## Literatura

Busque este libro en la biblioteca. Este libro ayudará a su hijo a reforzar los conceptos de más y menos.

**More, Fewer, Less** por Tana Hoban. Greenwillow Books, 1998.

© Houghton Mifflin Harcourt Publishing Company

Name _____

# Same Number

**COMMON CORE STANDARD** CC.K.CC.6
Compare numbers.

**❶**

_____

- - - - - - - - - - - - -

_____

_____

- - - - - - - - - - - - -

_____

**DIRECTIONS** **1.** Compare the sets of objects. Is the number of dolphins greater than, less than, or the same as the number of turtles? Count how many dolphins. Write the number. Count how many turtles. Write the number. Tell a friend what you know about the number of objects in each set.

**Chapter 2**

twenty-seven **P27**

# Lesson Check (CC.K.CC.6)

# Spiral Review (CC.K.CC.3, CC.K.CC.4a)

 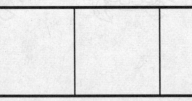 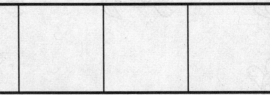

**DIRECTIONS** **I.** Which set shows the number of bears is the same as the number of cars? Mark under your answer. **(Lesson 2.1)** **2.** Which bird cage has 0 birds? Mark under your answer. **(Lesson 1.9)** **3.** Trace the number. How many counters would you place in the five frame to show the number? Mark under your answer. **(Lesson 1.1)**

Name _____

# Greater Than

COMMON CORE STANDARD CC.K.CC.6
Compare numbers.

**1**

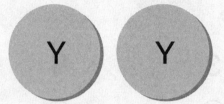

_____        _____

- - - - - - -          - - - - - - -

_____        _____

- - - - - - - - - - - - - - - - - - - - - - - - - - - - -

**2**

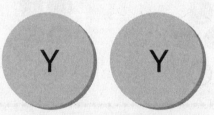

_____        _____

- - - - - - -          - - - - - - -

_____        _____

**DIRECTIONS   1–2.** Place counters as shown. Y is for yellow, and R is for red. Count and tell how many are in each set. Write the numbers. Compare the numbers. Circle the number that is greater.

**Chapter 2**

1     2     3     4

○     ○     ○     ○

## Spiral Review (CC.K.CC.4a)

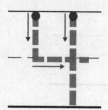 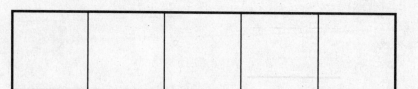

○     ○     ○     ○

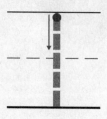 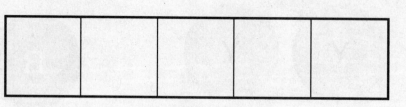

○     ○     ○     ○

**DIRECTIONS** **I.** Mark under the number that is greater than the number of counters. **(Lesson 2.2)** **2–3.** Trace the number. How many counters would you place in the five frame to show the number? Mark under your answer. **(Lessons 1.3, 1.1)**

Name _____

# Less Than

COMMON CORE STANDARD CC.K.CC.6
Compare numbers.

**1**

_____

- - - - -

_____

**2**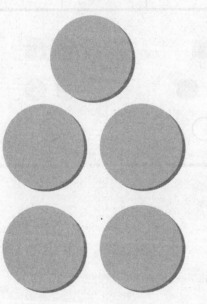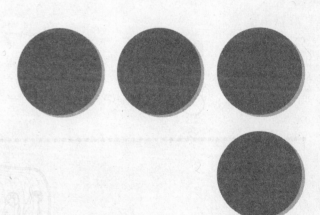

_____

- - - - -

_____

**DIRECTIONS** 1–2. Count and tell how many are in each set. Write the numbers. Compare the numbers. Circle the number that is less.

# Lesson Check (CC.K.CC.6)

**1**

| 2 | 3 | 4 | 5 |
|---|---|---|---|
| ○ | ○ | ○ | ○ |

# Spiral Review (CC.K.CC.4a, CC.K.CC.4b)

**2**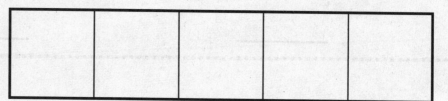

 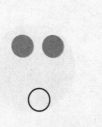 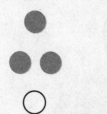 

○  ○  ○  ○

**3**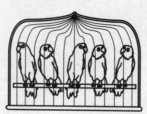

| 2 | 3 | 4 | 5 |
|---|---|---|---|
| ○ | ○ | ○ | ○ |

**DIRECTIONS** **1.** Mark under the number that is less than the number of counters. **(Lesson 2.3)** **2.** Trace the number. How many counters would you place in the five frame to show the number? Mark under your answer. **(Lesson 1.3)** **3.** Count how many birds. Mark under your answer. **(Lesson 1.6)**

Name _____

# Problem Solving • Compare by Matching Sets to 5

**COMMON CORE STANDARD** CC.K.CC.6
Compare numbers.

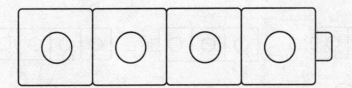

_____

- - - - - - - -

_____

_____

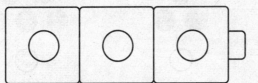

_____

- - - - - - - -

_____

_____

- - - - - - - -

_____

**DIRECTIONS** **1.** How many cubes are there? Write the number. Model a cube train that has a number of cubes greater than 4. Draw the cube train. Write how many. Compare the cube trains by matching. Tell a friend about the cube trains. **2.** How many cubes are there? Write the number. Model a cube train that has a number of cubes less than 3. Draw the cube train. Write how many. Compare the cube trains by matching. Tell a friend about the cube trains.

# Lesson Check (CC.K.CC.6)

    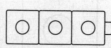  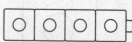

# Spiral Review (CC.K.CC.4.a)

  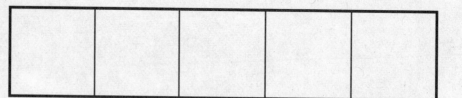

  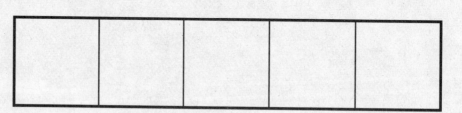

**DIRECTIONS** I. Which cube train has a number of cubes greater than 3? Mark under your answer. **(Lesson 2.4)** 2-3. Trace the number. How many counters would you place in the five frame to show the number? Mark under your answer. **(Lessons 1.5, 1.1)**

Name _____

# Compare by Counting Sets to 5

COMMON CORE STANDARD CC.K.CC.6
Compare numbers.

_____

_ _ _ _ _ _ _

_____

_____

_ _ _ _ _ _ _

_____

        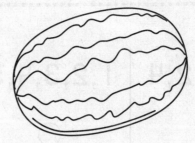

_____

_ _ _ _ _ _ _

_____

**DIRECTIONS**  1–2. Count how many objects are in each set. Write the numbers. Compare the numbers. Circle the number that is greater.  3. Count how many objects are in each set. Write the numbers. Compare the numbers. Circle the number that is less.

# Lesson Check (CC.K.CC.6)

**1**

| 1 | 2 | 3 | 4 |
|:-:|:-:|:-:|:-:|
| ○ | ○ | ○ | ○ |

# Spiral Review (CC.K.CC.3, CC.K.CC.4c)

**2**

| 1 | 2 | 3 | 4 |
|:-:|:-:|:-:|:-:|
| ○ | ○ | ○ | ○ |

**3**

| 5, 3, 1, 2, 4 | 1, 2, 3, 4, 5 | 3, 4, 5, 2, 1 | 1, 2, 5, 4, 3 |
|:-:|:-:|:-:|:-:|
| ○ | ○ | ○ | ○ |

**DIRECTIONS** **1.** Mark under the number that is less than the number of cars. (Lesson 2.5) **2.** Count and tell how many cats. Mark under your answer. (Lesson 1.4) **3.** Which set of numbers is in order? Mark under your answer. (Lesson 1.8)

Name _____

# Chapter 2 Extra Practice

## Lessons 2.1 – 2.2 (pp. 61–68) · · · · · · · · · · · · · · · · · · · · · · · · · ·

_____   _____

- - - - - - - - -   - - - - - - - - -

_____   _____

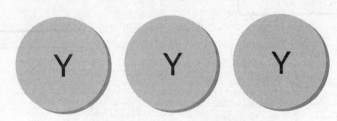   

_____   _____

- - - - - - - - -   - - - - - - - - -

_____   _____

**DIRECTIONS** 1. Compare the sets of objects. Is the number of lunch boxes greater than, less than, or the same as the number of backpacks? Count how many lunch boxes. Write the number. Count how many backpacks. Write the number. Tell a friend what you know about the number of objects in each set. **2.** Place counters as shown. Y is for yellow, and R is for red. Count and tell how many in each set. Write the numbers. Circle the number that is greater.

# Lessons 2.3 – 2.5 (pp. 69–80)

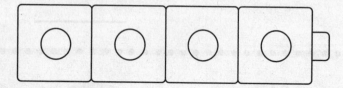

**DIRECTIONS** I. Count and tell how many in each set. Write the numbers. Compare the numbers. Circle the number that is less. **2.** How many cubes are there? Write the number. Model a cube train that has a number of cubes less than 4. Draw the cube train. Write how many. Compare the cube trains by matching. Tell a friend about the cube trains. **3.** Count how many objects in each set. Write the numbers. Compare the numbers. Circle the number that is greater.

# School-Home Letter

## Dear Family,

My class started Chapter 3 this week. In this chapter, I will learn how to show, count, and write numbers 6 to 9.

Love, _____

### Vocabulary

**six** one more than five

**eight** one more than seven

### Home Activity

Pour salt or sand into a cookie sheet or baking dish. Pick a number from 6 to 9 and have your child draw the number in the salt or sand. Then ask your child to draw circles to match that number. Shake to erase and begin again!

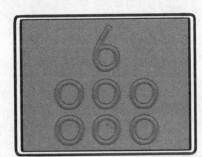

### Literature

Look for this book in the library. You and your child will enjoy this fun story that provides reinforcement of counting concepts.

**Seven Scary Monsters** by Mary Beth Lundgren. Clarion Books, 2003.

# Carta para la casa

## Querida familia:

Mi clase comenzó el Capítulo 3 esta semana. En este capítulo, aprenderé cómo mostrar, contar y escribir números del 6 al 9.

Con cariño, _____

## Vocabulario

**seis** uno más que cinco

**ocho** uno más que siete

## Actividad para la casa

Ponga sal o arena en una fuente para horno. Elija un número del 6 al 9 y pídale a su hijo que dibuje el número en la sal o la arena. Luego, pídale que dibuje el mismo número de círculos. Mezcle para borrar y ¡comiencen de nuevo!

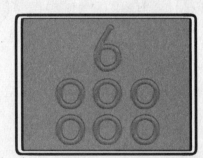

## Literatura

Busque este libro en la biblioteca. Usted y su hijo disfrutarán de este cuento divertido que proporciona un refuerzo para los conceptos de contar.

**Seven Scary Monsters**
por Mary Beth Lundgren.
Clarion Books, 2003.

Name _____

# Model and Count 6

COMMON CORE STANDARD CC.K.CC.5
Count to tell the number of objects.

**❶**

six

and

and

and

and

**DIRECTIONS  I.** Trace the number 6. Use two-color counters to model the different ways to make 6. Color to show the counters below. Write to show some pairs of numbers that make 6.

# Lesson Check (CC.K.CC.5)

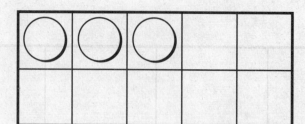

○          ○          ○          ○

# Spiral Review (CC.K.CC.3, CC.K.CC.6)

2          3          4          5
○          ○          ○          ○

1          2          3          4
○          ○          ○          ○

**DIRECTIONS** **1.** How many more counters would you place to model a way to make 6? Mark under your answer. **(Lesson 3.1)** **2.** Mark under the number that is less than the number of counters. **(Lesson 2.3)** **3.** How many cubes are there? Mark under your answer. **(Lesson 1.4)**

Name _____

# Count and Write 6

COMMON CORE STANDARD CC.K.CC.3
Know number names and the count sequence.

**1**

6 six    6 6 6 6 6 6 6

**2**

_____

- - - - - - - - -

_____

**3**

_____

- - - - - - - - -

_____

**4**

_____

- - - - - - - - -

_____

**5**

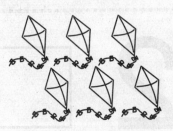

_____

- - - - - - - - -

_____

**DIRECTIONS** 1. Say the number. Trace the numbers.
**2–5.** Count and tell how many. Write the number.

# Lesson Check (CC.K.CC.3)

3      4      5      6

◯      ◯      ◯      ◯

# Spiral Review (CC.K.CC.4a, CC.K.CC.6)

1      2      3      4

◯      ◯      ◯      ◯

**2**
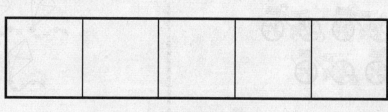

**DIRECTIONS** 1. How many school buses are there? Mark under your answer.
(Lesson 3.2) 2. Mark under the number that is greater than the number of
counters. (Lesson 2.2) 3. How many counters would you place in the five frame to
show the number? Mark under your answer. (Lesson 1.1)

# Model and Count 7

**COMMON CORE STANDARD CC.K.CC.5**
Count to tell the number of objects.

1.

7
**seven**

_ _ _ _ _ _ _          ◯          **and**          _ _ _ _ _ _ _          ◯

_ _ _ _ _ _ _          ◯          **and**          _ _ _ _ _ _ _          ◯

_ _ _ _ _ _ _          ◯          **and**          _ _ _ _ _ _ _          ◯

_ _ _ _ _ _ _          ◯          **and**          _ _ _ _ _ _ _          ◯

**DIRECTIONS** **I.** Trace the number 7. Use two-color counters
to model the different ways to make 7. Color to show the counters
below. Write to show some pairs of numbers that make 7.

**1**

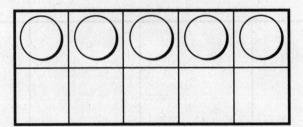

# Spiral Review (CC.K.CC.3, CC.K.CC.6)

**2**

| 1 | 2 | 3 | 4 |
|---|---|---|---|
| ○ | ○ | ○ | ○ |

**3**

| 1 | 2 | 3 | 4 |
|---|---|---|---|
| ○ | ○ | ○ | ○ |

**DIRECTIONS 1.** How many more counters would you place to model a way to make 7? Mark under your answer. **(Lesson 3.3) 2.** Mark under the number that is less than the number of counters. **(Lesson 2.3) 3.** How many birds are there? Mark under your answer. **(Lesson 1.4)**

# Count and Write 7

COMMON CORE STANDARD CC.K.CC.3
Know number names and the
count sequence.

**1**

# 7
## seven

7  7  7  7  7  7  7

---

**2**

_____

- - - - - - - - -

_____

**3**

_____

- - - - - - - - -

_____

---

**4**

_____

- - - - - - - - -

_____

**5**

_____

- - - - - - - - -

_____

---

**DIRECTIONS** 1. Say the number. Trace the numbers.
**2–5.** Count and tell how many. Write the number.

## Lesson Check (CC.K.CC.3)

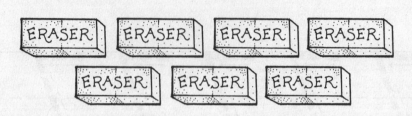

| 4 | 5 | 6 | 7 |
| :-: | :-: | :-: | :-: |
| ○ | ○ | ○ | ○ |

## Spiral Review (CC.K.CC.3, CC.K.CC.4a)

**3**

| | | | |
| :-: | :-: | :-: | :-: |

| ○ | ○ | ○ | ○ |
| :-: | :-: | :-: | :-: |

**2**

| ○ | ○ | ○ | ○ |
| :-: | :-: | :-: | :-: |

**DIRECTIONS** **1.** Count and tell how many erasers. Mark under your answer.
**(Lesson 3.4)** **2.** How many counters would you place in the five frame to show the number? Mark under your answer. **(Lesson 1.3)** **3.** Which set shows the number? Mark under your answer. **(Lesson 1.2)**

Name _____

# Model and Count 8

**COMMON CORE STANDARD CC.K.CC.5**
Count to tell the number of objects.

8
**eight**

_ _ _ _ _ _   ⃝   **and**   _____   ⃝

_ _ _ _ _ _   ⃝   **and**   _____   ⃝

_ _ _ _ _ _   ⃝   **and**   _____   ⃝

_ _ _ _ _ _   ⃝   **and**   _____   ⃝

**DIRECTIONS   I.** Trace the number 8. Use two-color counters
to model the different ways to make 8. Color to show the counters
below. Write to show some pairs of numbers that make 8.

## Lesson Check (CC.K.CC.5)

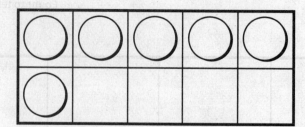

○                    ○                    ○                    ○

## Spiral Review (CC.K.CC.3, CC.K.CC.6)

○                    ○                    ○                    ○

| 1 | 2 | 3 | 4 |

○                    ○                    ○                    ○

**DIRECTIONS** 1. How many more counters would you place to model a way to make 8? Mark under your answer. (Lesson 3.5)  2. Which cube train has a number of cubes greater than 4? Mark under your answer. (Lesson 2.4)  3. Count and tell how many stop signs. Mark under your answer. (Lesson 1.2)

# Count and Write 8

**1**

**8**
eight

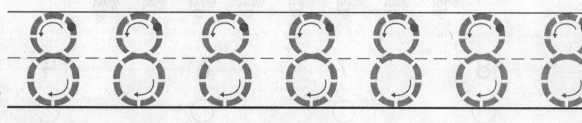

**2**

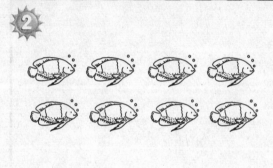

_____
- - - - - -
_____

**3**

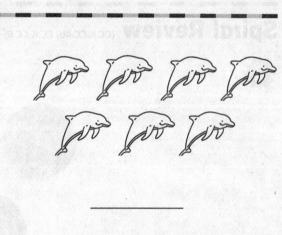

_____
- - - - - -
_____

**4**

_____
- - - - - -
_____

**5**

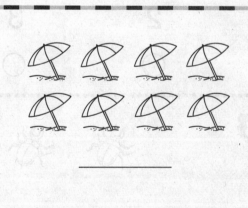

_____
- - - - - -
_____

**DIRECTIONS** 1. Say the number. Trace the numbers.
**2–5.** Count and tell how many. Write the number.

## Lesson Check (CC.K.CC.3)

| 8 | 7 | 6 | 4 |
|---|---|---|---|
| ○ | ○ | ○ | ○ |

## Spiral Review (CC.K.CC.4b, CC.K.CC.6)

| 2 | 3 | 4 | 5 |
|---|---|---|---|
| ○ | ○ | ○ | ○ |

| two | three | four | five |
|---|---|---|---|
|  |  | ○ | ○ |

**DIRECTIONS** 1. Count and tell how many bees. Mark under your answer. **(Lesson 3.6)**
2. Mark under the number that is greater than the number of counters. **(Lesson 2.2)**
3. Count and tell how many beetles. Mark under your answer. **(Lesson 1.6)**

# Model and Count 9

COMMON CORE STANDARD CC.K.CC.5
Count to tell the number of objects.

❶

nine

_____  ⬤  **and**  _____  ⬤

_____  ⬤  **and**  _____  ⬤

_____  ⬤  **and**  _____  ⬤

_____  ⬤  **and**  _____  ⬤

**DIRECTIONS** I. Trace the number 9. Use two-color counters to model the different ways to make 9. Color to show the counters below. Write to show some pairs of numbers that make 9.

# Lesson Check (CC.K.CC.5)

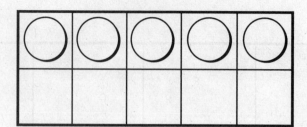

# Spiral Review (CC.K.CC.3, CC.K.CC.6)

1        2        3        4

○        ○        ○        ○

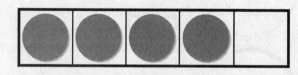

1        2        3        4

○        ○        ○        ○

**DIRECTIONS** 1. How many more counters would you place to model a way to make 9? Mark under your answer. (Lesson 3.7) 2. Mark under the number that is greater than the number of cats. (Lesson 2.5) 3. How many counters are there? Mark under your answer. (Lesson 1.4)

# Count and Write 9

COMMON CORE STANDARD CC.K.CC.3
Know number names and the
count sequence.

**1**

# 9
**nine**  9 9 9 9 9 9 9

**2**

_ _ _ _ _ _ _ _

- - - - - - - -

_____

**3**

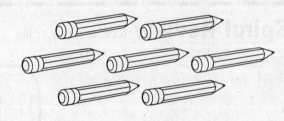

_ _ _ _ _ _ _ _

- - - - - - - -

_____

**4**

_ _ _ _ _ _ _ _

- - - - - - - -

_____

**5**

_ _ _ _ _ _ _ _

- - - - - - - -

_____

**DIRECTIONS** **1.** Say the number. Trace the numbers.
**2–5.** Count and tell how many. Write the number.

## Lesson Check (CC.K.CC.3)

**1**

six      seven      eight      nine

○      ○      ○      ○

## Spiral Review (CC.K.CC.3, CC.K.CC.4b)

**2**

0      1      2      3

○      ○      ○      ○

**3**

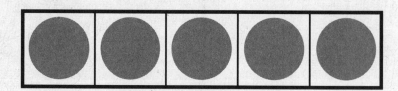

2      3      4      5

○      ○      ○      ○

**DIRECTIONS**   1. Count and tell how many squirrels. Mark under your answer.
(Lesson 3.8)   2. How many birds are in the cage? Mark under your answer.
(Lesson 1.10)   3. How many counters are there? Mark under your answer.   (Lesson 1.6)

Name _____

## Problem Solving • Numbers to 9

COMMON CORE STANDARD CC.K.CC.6
Compare numbers.

_____

- - - - - - -

_____

_____

- - - - - - -

_____

_____

- - - - - - -

_____

_____

- - - - - - -

_____

**DIRECTIONS** **1.** Sally has six flowers. Three of the flowers are yellow. The rest are red. How many are yellow? Draw the flowers. Write the number beside each set of flowers. **2.** Tim has seven acorns. Don has a number of acorns that is two less than 7. How many acorns does Don have? Draw the acorns. Write the numbers.

# Lesson Check (CC.K.CC.6)

2       3       5       7

◯       ◯       ◯       ◯

# Spiral Review (CC.K.CC.4b, CC.K.CC.6)

2       3       4       5

◯       ◯       ◯       ◯

2       3       4       5

◯       ◯       ◯       ◯

**DIRECTIONS** **1.** The house has five doors. The number of windows is two more than 5. How many windows are there? Mark under your answer. **(Lesson 3.9)** **2.** Count and tell how many books. Mark your answer. **(Lesson 1.6)** **3.** Mark under the number that is greater than the number of turtles. **(Lesson 2.5)**

COMMON CORE STANDARDS CC.K.CC.3, CC.K.CC.5, CC.K.CC.6

# Chapter 3 Extra Practice

## Lessons 3.1 – 3.6 (pp. 89–112)

**1**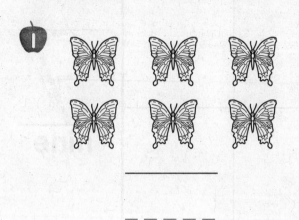

_____

_ _ _ _ _

_____

**2**

_____

_ _ _ _ _

_____

**3**

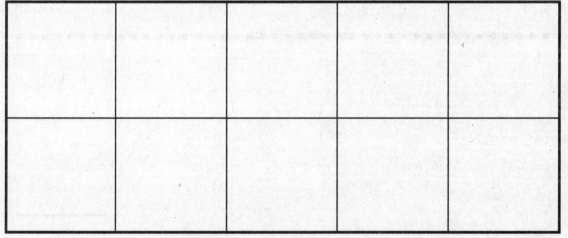

eight

_____ ⬭ and _____ ⬭

**DIRECTIONS** 1–2. Count and tell how many. Write the number. **3.** Trace the number 8. Use two-color counters to model a way to make 8. Color to show the counters below. Write to show a pair of numbers that makes 8.

**❶**

9
nine

_____  ⭕  **and**  _____  ⭕

**②**

_____

- - - - - - -

_____

_____

- - - - - - -

_____

**DIRECTIONS  I.** Trace the number 9. Use two-color counters to model a way to make 9. Color to show the counters below. Write to show a pair of numbers that makes 9.  **2.** Roy has seven spoons. Ken has a number of spoons two greater than 7. Draw the spoons. Write the numbers.

© Houghton Mifflin Harcourt Publishing Company

# School-Home Letter

## Dear Family,

My class started Chapter 4 this week. In this chapter, I will learn how to show and compare numbers to 10.

Love, _____

## Vocabulary

**ten** one more than nine

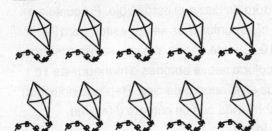

## Home Activity

Place one button or penny in the ten frame below. Ask your child how many more are needed to make 10. Count aloud with your child as he or she places nine more buttons or pennies in the ten frame. Repeat the activity, starting with a different number each time.

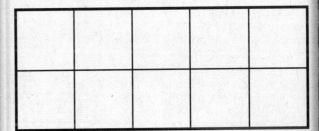

## Literature

Look for these books in the library. You and your child will enjoy these fun stories while learning more about the numbers 6 to 10.

**Feast for 10** by Cathryn Falwell. Clarion Books, 1993.

**Ten Black Dots** by Donald Crews. Greenwillow Books, 1995.

# Carta
## para la casa

## Querida familia:

Mi clase comenzó el Capítulo 4 esta semana. En este capítulo, aprenderé mostrar y comparar números hasta el 10.

Con cariño, _____

## Vocabulario

**diez** uno más que nueve

## Actividad para la casa

Ponga un botón o una moneda de 1¢ en el cuadro de diez que está abajo. Pregúntele a su hijo cuántos más se necesitan para llegar a 10. Cuente en voz alta con su hijo mientras él coloca nueve botones o monedas de 1¢ más en el cuadro de diez. Repita la actividad y comience con un número diferente cada vez.

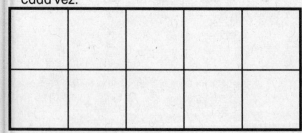

## Literatura

Busquen estos libros en la biblioteca. Usted y su hijo se divertirán leyendo estos cuentos mientras aprenden más sobre los números del 6 al 10.

**Feast for 10** by Cathryn Falwell. Clarion Books, 1993.

**Ten Black Dots** by Donald Crews. Greenwillow Books, 1995.

# Model and Count 10

**COMMON CORE STANDARD** CC.K.CC.5
Count to tell the number of objects.

**ten**

_____ _____ _____ **and** _____ _____

_____ _____ _____ **and** _____ _____

_____ _____ _____ **and** _____ _____

_____ _____ _____ **and** _____ _____

**DIRECTIONS**  Trace the number. Use counters to model the different ways to make 10. Color to show the counters below. Write to show some pairs of numbers that make 10.

**Chapter 4**

# Lesson Check (CC.K.CC.5)

**1**

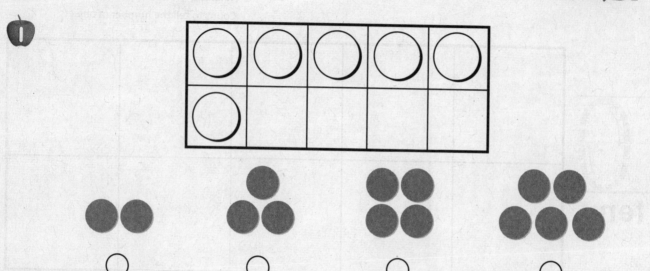

# Spiral Review (CC.K.CC.6, CC.K.CC.3)

**2**

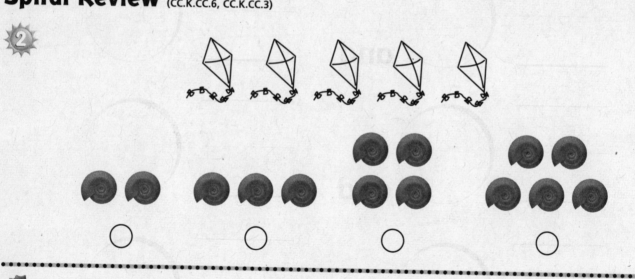

**3**

4          3          2          1

○          ○          ○          ○

**DIRECTIONS  1.** How many more counters would you place to model a way to make 10? Mark under your answer. **(Lesson 4.1)**  **2.** Mark under the set that has the same number of objects as the set of kites. **(Lesson 2.1)**  **3.** Count and tell how many coats. Mark under your answer. **(Lesson 1.2)**

Name _____

# Count and Write 10

COMMON CORE STANDARD CC.K.CC.3
Know number names and the count sequence.

**❶**

**10**
**ten**

10 10 10 10 10

**❷**

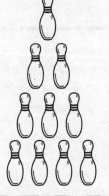

_____

- - - - - - - - - - - - - -

_____

**❸**

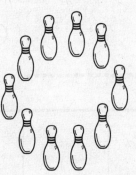

_____

- - - - - - - - - - - - - -

_____

**❹**

_____

- - - - - - - - - - - - - -

_____

**DIRECTIONS** **1.** Say the number. Trace the numbers.
**2–4.** Count and tell how many. Write the number.

## Lesson Check (CC.K.CC.3)

**1**

| seven | eight | nine | ten |
|:---:|:---:|:---:|:---:|
| ○ | ○ | ○ | ○ |

## Spiral Review (CC.K.CC.6, CC.K.CC.4a)

| 2 | 3 | 4 | 5 |
|:---:|:---:|:---:|:---:|
| ○ | ○ | ○ | ○ |

5

| | | | | |
|---|---|---|---|---|

| ○ | ○ | ○ | ○ |
|:---:|:---:|:---:|:---:|

**DIRECTIONS** 1. Count and tell how many ears of corn. Mark under your answer.
(Lesson 4.2) 2. Mark under the number that is less than the number of counters.
(Lesson 2.3) 3. How many counters would you place in the five frame to show the number?
Mark under your answer. (Lesson 1.5)

# Algebra • Ways to Make 10

**COMMON CORE STANDARD** CC.K.OA.4
Understand addition as putting together and adding to, and understand subtraction as taking apart and taking from.

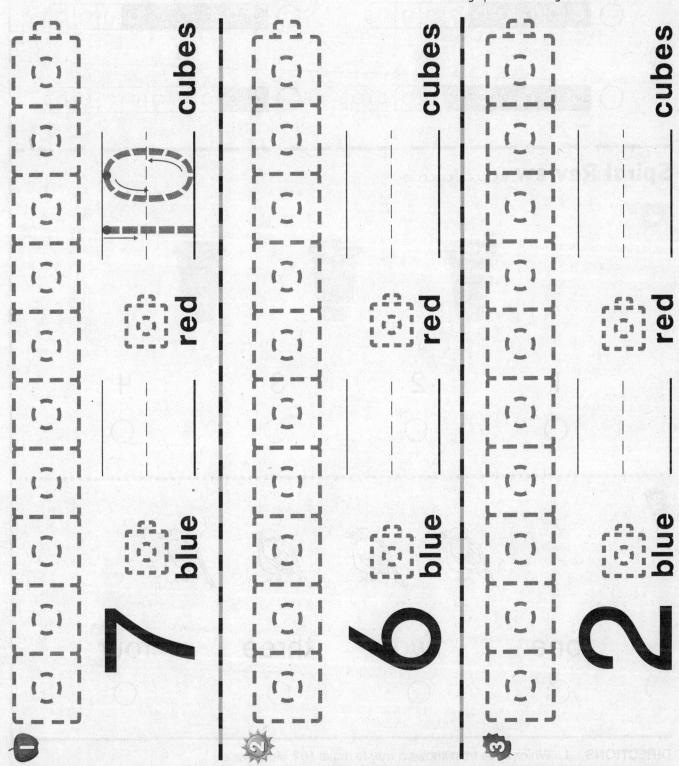

**DIRECTIONS** 1–3. Use blue to color the cubes to match the number. Use red to color the other cubes. Write how many red cubes. Trace or write the number that shows how many cubes in all.

## Lesson Check (CC.K.OA.4)

○ [cube train]    ○ [cube train]

○ [cube train]    ○ [cube train]

## Spiral Review (CC.K.CC.6, CC.K.CC.3)

1        2        3        4

○        ○        ○        ○

one      two      three      four

○        ○        ○        ○

---

**DIRECTIONS 1.** Which cube train shows a way to make 10? Mark beside your answer. (Lesson 4.3) **2.** Mark under the number that is greater than the number of cups. (Lesson 2.5) **3.** How many birds are there? Mark under your answer. (Lesson 1.4)

## Count and Order to 10

COMMON CORE STANDARD CC.K.CC.2
Know number names and the count sequence.

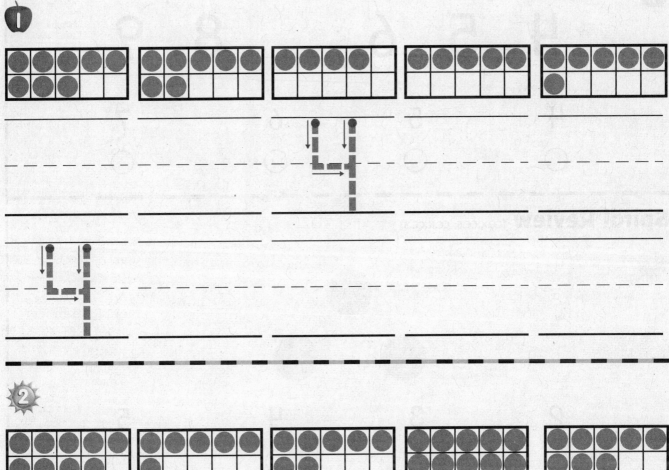

**DIRECTIONS** **1–2.** Count the dots in the ten frames. Trace or write the numbers. Write the numbers in order as you count forward from the dashed number.

4   5   6   ___   8   9

4       5       6       7
○       ○       ○       ○

**Spiral Review** (CC.K.CC.6, CC.K.CC.3)

2       3       4       5
○       ○       ○       ○

4       3       2       1
four    three   two     one
○       ○       ○       ○

**DIRECTIONS**  **1.** Count forward. Mark under the number that fills the space. **(Lesson 4.4)**  **2.** Mark under the number that is less than the number of counters. **(Lesson 2.3)**  **3.** How many counters are there? Mark under your answer. **(Lesson 1.4)**

## Problem Solving • Compare by Matching Sets to 10

**COMMON CORE STANDARD** CC.K.CC.6
Compare numbers.

1

_____

- - - - - - -

_____

- - - - - - -

_____

---

2

_____

- - - - - - -

_____

_____

- - - - - - -

_____

---

**DIRECTIONS** **1.** Kim has 7 red balloons. Jake has 3 blue balloons. Who has fewer balloons? Use cube trains to model the sets of balloons. Compare the cube trains. Write how many. Circle the number that is less. **2.** Meg has 8 red beads. Beni has 5 blue beads. Who has more beads? Use cube trains to model the sets of beads. Compare the cube trains by matching. Draw and color the cube trains. Write how many. Circle the number that is greater.

## Lesson Check (CC.K.CC.6)

○ ▢▢▢▢▢▢▢

○ ▢▢▢▢▢▢▢

○ ▢▢▢▢▢▢▢▢

○ ▢▢▢▢▢▢

## Spiral Review (CC.K.CC.6, CC.K.CC.4b)

| 1 | 2 | 3 | 4 |
|---|---|---|---|
| ○ | ○ | ○ | ○ |

**5**

   ○

**DIRECTIONS  1.** Compare the cube trains by matching. Mark beside the cube train that has a greater number of cubes. **(Lesson 4.5)  2.** Mark under the number that is greater than the number of counters. **(Lesson 2.2)**
**3.** Which set shows the number? Mark under your answer. **(Lesson 1.6)**

Name _____

# Compare by Counting Sets to 10

**COMMON CORE STANDARD** CC.K.CC.6
Compare numbers.

_____

- - - - - - - - - - -

_____

- - - - - - - - - - -        _____

_____        - - - - - - - - - - -

_____        _____

- - - - - - - - - - -        - - - - - - - - - - -

_____        _____

        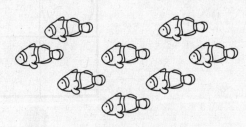

_____        _____

- - - - - - - - - - -        - - - - - - - - - - -

_____        _____

**DIRECTIONS** Count how many in each set. Write the number of objects in each set. Compare the numbers.   **1–2.** Circle the number that is less.   **3.** Circle the number that is greater.

**Chapter 4**        seventy-three **P73**

# Lesson Check (CC.K.CC.6)

| 6 | 7 | 8 | 9 |
|:---:|:---:|:---:|:---:|
| ○ | ○ | ○ | ○ |

# Spiral Review (CC.K.CC.3, CC.K.CC.5)

| 5 | 6 | 7 | 8 |
|:---:|:---:|:---:|:---:|
| ○ | ○ | ○ | ○ |

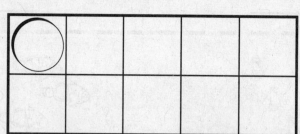

| ○ | ○ | ○ | ○ |
|:---:|:---:|:---:|:---:|

---

**DIRECTIONS  1.** Mark under the number that is less than the number of pencils.
**(Lesson 4.6)  2.** Count and tell how many whistles. Mark under your answer.  **(Lesson 3.6)**
**3.** How many more counters would you place to model a way to make 6?  **(Lesson 3.1)**

# Compare Two Numbers

**COMMON CORE STANDARD** CC.K.CC.7
Compare numbers.

**1**    8                    5

---

**2**    10                   7

---

**3**    6                    9

---

**4**    4                    6

---

**5**    8                    7

---

**6**    5                    3

---

**DIRECTIONS**    1–3. Look at the numbers. Think about the counting order as you compare the numbers. Circle the greater number.    4–6. Look at the numbers. Think about the counting order as you compare the numbers. Circle the number that is less.

## Lesson Check (CC.K.CC.7)

**1**

# 7

6         8         I         5

○         ○         ○         ○

## Spiral Review (CC.K.CC.5, CC.K.CC.3)

**2**

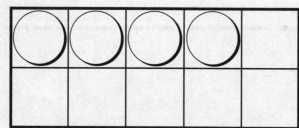

○         ○         ○         ○

**3**

six      seven      eight      nine

○         ○         ○         ○

**DIRECTIONS** 1. Which number is greater than 7? Mark under your answer. (Lesson 4.7)
2. How many more counters would you place to model a way to make 8? Mark under your answer. (Lesson 3.5) 3. Count and tell how many birds. Mark under your answer. (Lesson 3.8)

COMMON CORE STANDARDS CC.K.CC.2, CC.K.CC.3, CC.K.CC.5, CC.K.CC.6, CC.K.CC.7, CC.K.OA.4

# Chapter 4 Extra Practice

## Lessons 4.1–4.4 (pp. 133–147) · · · · · · · · · · · · · · · · · · · · · ·

_____

- - - - - - - - - - -

_____

● ● ● ● ● ● ● ● ● ● ● ● ● ● ● ● ● ● ● ● ● ● ● ● ● ● ● ● ● ●

**3**  blue  _ _ _ _ _ _  red  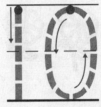 cubes

● ● ● ● ● ● ● ● ● ● ● ● ● ● ● ● ● ● ● ● ● ● ● ● ● ● ● ● ● ●

## 6, 8, 5, 7, 9

**5** _____  _____  _____  _____

- - - - - -  - - - - - -  - - - - - -  - - - - - -

_____  _____  _____  _____

**DIRECTIONS** 1. Count and tell how many balloons. Write the number.
2. Use blue to color the cubes to match the number. Use red to color the
other cubes. Write how many red cubes. Trace the number that shows how
many cubes in all. 3. Write the numbers in order as you count forward from 5.

**1**

---

**2**

_____

- - - - - - -

_____

- - - - - - -

_____

---

## 8          4

---

**DIRECTIONS  1.** Pam has 9 red crayons. Alex has 7 blue crayons. Who has more crayons? Use cube trains to model the sets of crayons. Compare the cube trains by matching. Draw and color the cube trains. Write how many. Circle the number that is greater.  **2.** Count how many in each set. Write the number of objects in each set. Compare the numbers. Circle the number that is less.  **3.** Think about the counting order as you compare the numbers. Circle the greater number.

# School-Home Letter

## Dear Family,

My class started Chapter 5 this week. In this chapter, I will learn how to show addition.

Love, _____

## Vocabulary

**add** to put together one set with another set

○ ○ ○ ○ ○ ○

**plus (+)** a symbol that shows addition

plus
↓
$3 + 2 = 5$

## Home Activity

Invite your child to act out addition word problems. For example, your child can show you four socks, add two more socks, and then tell you the addition sentence.

$4 + 2 = 6$

## Literature

Look for these books at the library. You and your child will enjoy counting and adding objects in these interactive books.

**Rooster's Off to See the World** by Eric Carle. Simon & Schuster, 1991.

**Anno's Counting Book** by Mitsumasa Anno. HarperCollins, 1986.

# Carta
## para la casa

## Querida familia:

Mi clase comenzó el Capítulo 5 esta semana. En este capítulo aprenderé todo sobre la suma.

Con cariño, _____

## Vocabulario

**sumar** agregar un conjunto a otro

⬛⬛⬛◻◻

**más (+)** signo que indica suma

más
↓
3 + 2 = 5

## Actividad para la casa

Anime a su hijo a representar problemas de suma. Por ejemplo, puede mostrar cuatro calcetines, agregar dos calcetines más y luego decir el enunciado de la suma.

4 + 2 = 6

Busquen otros objetos que puedan usarse para representar cuentos de resta.

## Literatura

Busquen estos libros en la biblioteca. Usted y su hijo disfrutarán estos libros interactivos que sirven para reforzar las destrezas de suma.

**Rooster's Off to See the World**
por Eric Carle. Simon & Schuster, 1991.

**Anno's Counting Book**
by Mitsumasa Anno. HarperCollins, 1986.

Name _____

# Addition: Add To

**COMMON CORE STANDARD** CC.K.OA.1
Understand addition as putting together and adding to, and understand subtraction as taking apart and taking from.

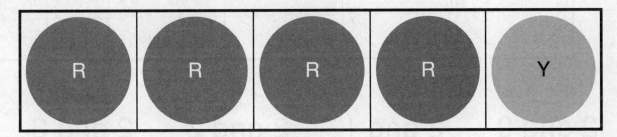

_____            _____

- - - -  **and**  - - - -

_____            _____

- - - - - - - - - - - - - - - - - - - - - - - - - - - -

_____

- - - - -

_____

---

**DIRECTIONS** **1.** There are four red counters in the five frame. One yellow counter is added. R is for red, and Y is for yellow. How many of each color counter? Write the numbers. **2.** Write the number that shows how many counters are in the five frame now.

# Lesson Check (CC.K.OA.1)

 **1**

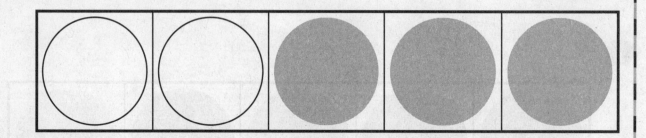

| 2 and 0 | 2 and 1 | 2 and 2 | 2 and 3 |
| :---: | :---: | :---: | :---: |
| ○ | ○ | ○ | ○ |

## Spiral Review (CC.K.CC.3, CC.K.CC.6)

 **2**

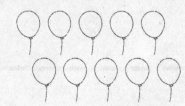

| 7 | 8 | 9 | 10 |
| :---: | :---: | :---: | :---: |
| ○ | ○ | ○ | ○ |

 **3**

| 2 | 3 | 4 | 5 |
| :---: | :---: | :---: | :---: |
| ○ | ○ | ○ | ○ |

**DIRECTIONS** 1. Which shows the gray counters being added to the five frame? Mark under your answer. (Lesson 5.1) 2. Count and tell how many balloons. Mark under your answer. (Lesson 4.2) 3. Mark under the number that is less than the number of shells. (Lesson 2.5)

# Addition: Put Together

**COMMON CORE STANDARD CC.K.OA.1**
Understand addition as putting together
and adding to, and understand subtraction
as taking apart and taking from.

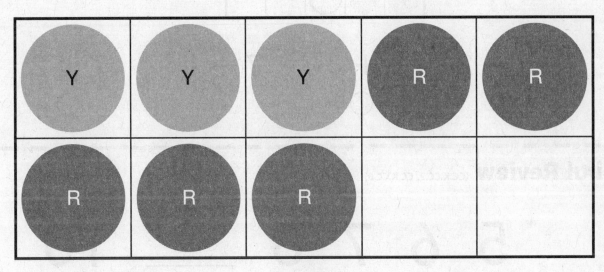

**3**        **and**        **5**

_ _ _ _ _        ┼        _ _ _ _ _

_____        _ _ _ _        _____

---

**DIRECTIONS**  Roy has three yellow counters and five red counters. How
many counters does he have in all? **I.** Place counters in the ten frame to
model the sets that are put together. Y is for yellow, and R is for red. Write
the numbers and trace the symbol. Write the number to show how many in all.

## Lesson Check (CC.K.OA.1)

$5 + 2$     $5 + 3$     $7 + 1$     $7 + 2$

◯      ◯      ◯      ◯

## Spiral Review (CC.K.CC.2, CC.K.CC.6)

# 5  6  7  8  ____  10

6      7      8      9

◯      ◯      ◯      ◯

**3**

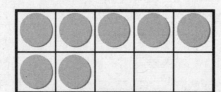

5      6      7      9

◯      ◯      ◯      ◯

**DIRECTIONS** **1.** Which numbers show the sets that are put together? Mark under your answer. **(Lesson 5.2)** **2.** Count forward. Mark under the number that fills the space. **(Lesson 4.4)** **3.** Meg has seven counters. Paul has a number of counters two less than seven. Mark under the number that shows how many counters Paul has. **(Lesson 3.9)**

Name _____

# Problem Solving • Act Out
# Addition Problems

**COMMON CORE STANDARD CC.K.OA.1**
Understand addition as putting together
and adding to, and understand subtraction
as taking apart and taking from.

**1**

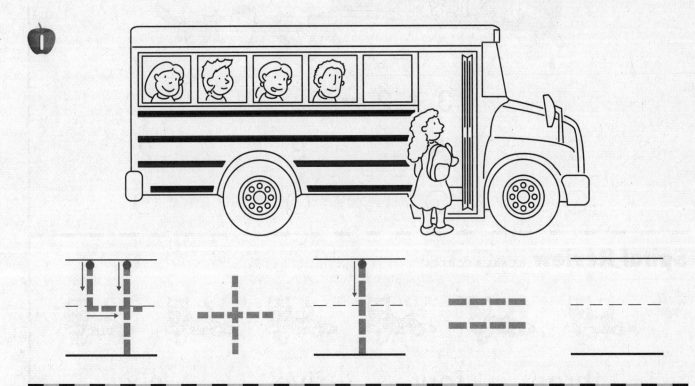

4 + 1 = ___

**2**

3 + 2 = ___

**DIRECTIONS 1–2.** Tell an addition word problem about the
children. Trace the numbers and the symbols. Write the number that
shows how many children in all.

## Lesson Check (CC.K.OA.1)

$$3 + 2 = \underline{\hspace{2cm}}$$

| 5 | 4 | 3 | 2 |
|---|---|---|---|
| ◯ | ◯ | ◯ | ◯ |

## Spiral Review (CC.K.CC.3, CC.K.CC.6)

| three | four | five | six |
|-------|------|------|-----|
| ◯ | ◯ | ◯ | ◯ |

| ◯ | ◯ | ◯ | ◯ |
|---|---|---|---|

**DIRECTIONS** **I.** How many cats are there in all? Mark under your answer. **(Lesson 5.3)**
**2.** Count and tell how many tigers. Mark under your answer. **(Lesson 3.2)** **3.** Mark under
the set that has the same number of objects. **(Lesson 2.1)**

# Algebra • Model and Draw
# Addition Problems

**COMMON CORE STANDARD** CC.K.OA.5
Understand addition as putting together and adding to, and understand subtraction as taking apart and taking from.

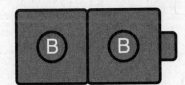 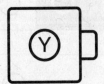

  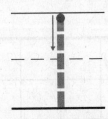

$$2 + 1 = \underline{\phantom{000}}$$

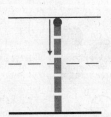   

$$1 + 3 = \underline{\phantom{000}}$$

**DIRECTIONS    1–2.** Place cubes as shown. B is for blue, and Y is for yellow. Tell an addition word problem. Model to show the cubes put together. Draw the cube train. Trace and write to complete the addition sentence.

# Lesson Check (CC.K.OA.5)

$\bigcirc \; 2 + 1 = 3$        $\bigcirc \; 3 + 1 = 4$

$\bigcirc \; 2 + 3 = 5$        $\bigcirc \; 3 + 2 = 5$

# Spiral Review (CC.K.CC.3, CC.K.CC.5)

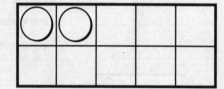

        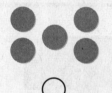

**DIRECTIONS** **1.** Which addition sentence shows the cubes being put together? Mark beside your answer. **(Lesson 5.4)** **2.** How many more counters would you place to model a way to make 7? Mark under your answer. **(Lesson 3.3)** **3.** Mark under the set that shows the number. **(Lesson 1.4)**

# Algebra • Write Addition Sentences for 10

COMMON CORE STANDARD CC.K.OA.4
Understand addition as putting together
and adding to, and understand subtraction
as taking apart and taking from.

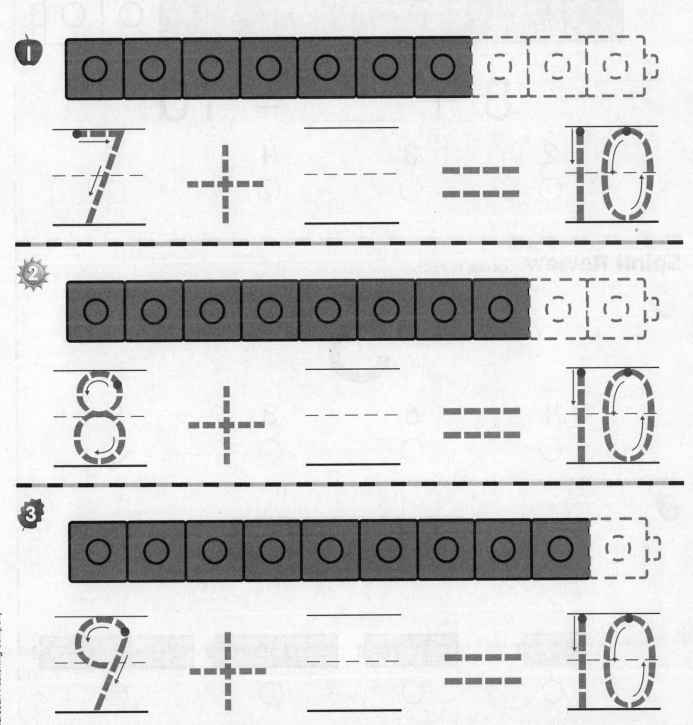

**1**    7 + ___ = 10

**2**    8 + ___ = 10

**3**    9 + ___ = 10

**DIRECTIONS**    1–3. Look at the cube train. How many gray cubes do you
see? How many blue cubes do you need to add to make 10? Use blue to
color those cubes. Write and trace to show this as an addition sentence.

## Lesson Check (CC.K.OA.4)

 1

$$8 + \underline{\phantom{xx}} = 10$$

2      3      4      5

○      ○      ○      ○

## Spiral Review (CC.K.CC.6, CC.K.CC.7)

2

# 5

4      6      8      9

○      ○      ○      ○

 3

        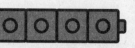   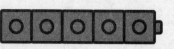

○      ○      ○      ○

**DIRECTIONS** **1.** Mark under the number that makes 10 when put together with the given number. **(Lesson 5.5)** **2.** Which number is less than 5? Mark under your answer. **(Lesson 4.7)** **3.** Which cube train has the same number of cubes? Mark under your answer. **(Lesson 2.4)**

**P90** ninety

Name _____

# Algebra • Write Addition Sentences

**COMMON CORE STANDARD** CC.K.OA.5
Understand addition as putting together and adding to, and understand subtraction as taking apart and taking from.

3 + ___ = 5

1 + ___ = 4

4 + ___ = 5

**DIRECTIONS 1–3.** Tell an addition word problem about the sets. Circle the set you start with. How many are being added to the set? How many are there now? Write and trace to complete the addition sentence.

# Lesson Check (CC.K.OA.5)

 **1**

$$3 + \underline{\quad} = 5$$

| 1 | 2 | 3 | 4 |
|---|---|---|---|
| ○ | ○ | ○ | ○ |

# Spiral Review (CC.K.CC.3, CC.K.CC.5)

 **2**

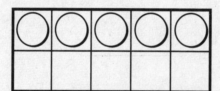

○          ○          ○          ○

 **3**

| 1 | 2 | 3 | 4 |
|---|---|---|---|
| ○ | ○ | ○ | ○ |

**DIRECTIONS** **1.** Which number completes the addition sentence about the sets of airplanes? Mark under your answer. **(Lesson 5.6)** **2.** How many more counters would you place to model a way to make 8? Mark under your answer. **(Lesson 3.5)** **3.** How many paintbrushes are there? Mark under your answer. **(Lesson 1.4)**

# Algebra • Write More Addition Sentences

**COMMON CORE STANDARD** CC.K.OA.2
Understand addition as putting together and adding to, and understand subtraction as taking apart and taking from.

____
____ + 5 === 9

____
____ + 4 === 10

____
____ + 4 === 7

____
____ + 3 === 8

**DIRECTIONS   1–4.** Tell an addition word problem. Circle the set being added. How many are in the set to start with? Write and trace to complete the addition sentence.

# Lesson Check (CC.K.OA.2)

## ___ + 3 = 9

| 3 | 4 | 5 | 6 |
|---|---|---|---|
| ○ | ○ | ○ | ○ |

# Spiral Review (CC.K.CC.4b, CC.K.CC.5)

 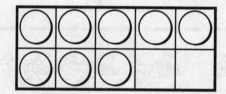

| ○ | ○ | ○ | ○ |
|---|---|---|---|

| 2 | 3 | 4 | 5 |
|---|---|---|---|
| ○ | ○ | ○ | ○ |

**DIRECTIONS** **1.** Which number completes the addition sentence about the sets of dogs? Mark under your answer. (Lesson 5.7)  **2.** How many more counters would you place to model a way to make 9? Mark under your answer. (Lesson 3.7)  **3.** Count and tell how many trumpets. Mark under your answer. (Lesson 1.6)

Name _____

# Algebra • Number Pairs to 5

**COMMON CORE STANDARD** CC.K.OA.3
Understand addition as putting together and adding to, and understand subtraction as taking apart and taking from.

**1**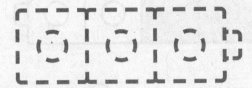

$3$ $=$ $\underline{\hspace{1cm}}$ $+$ $\underline{\hspace{1cm}}$

**2**

$4$ $=$ $\underline{\hspace{1cm}}$ $+$ $\underline{\hspace{1cm}}$

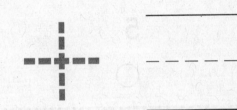

**3**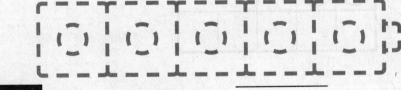

$5$ $=$ $\underline{\hspace{1cm}}$ $+$ $\underline{\hspace{1cm}}$

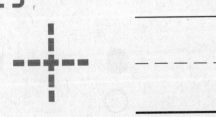

**DIRECTIONS** 1–3. Look at the number at the beginning of the addition sentence. Place two colors of cubes on the cube train to show a number pair for that number. Complete the addition sentence to show a number pair. Color the cube train to match the addition sentence.

## Lesson Check (CC.K.OA.3)

○ 5 = 1 + 4      ○ 6 = 1 + 5

○ 5 = 3 + 2      ○ 6 = 2 + 4

## Spiral Review (CC.K.CC.5, CC.K.CC.6)

5      6      7      8

○      ○      ○      ○

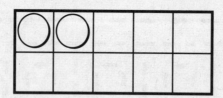

○      ○      ○      ○

**DIRECTIONS** **1.** Which addition sentence shows a pair of numbers that matches the cube train? Mark beside your answer. (Lesson 5.8) **2.** Mark under the number that is greater than the number of turtles. (Lesson 4.6) **3.** How many more counters would you place to model a way to make 6? Mark under your answer (Lesson 3.1)

Name _____

# Algebra • Number Pairs for 6 and 7

**COMMON CORE STANDARD** CC.K.OA.3
Understand addition as putting together
and adding to, and understand subtraction
as taking apart and taking from.

$$6 = \underline{\quad\quad} + \underline{\quad\quad}$$

---

$$7 = \underline{\quad\quad} + \underline{\quad\quad}$$

**DIRECTIONS  I–2.** Look at the number at the beginning of the addition
sentence. Place two colors of cubes on the cube train to show a number
pair for that number. Complete the addition sentence to show a number
pair. Color the cube train to match the addition sentence.

**Chapter 5**

## Lesson Check (CC.K.OA.3)

**1**

○ 6 = 1 + 5          ○ 7 = 1 + 6

○ 6 = 2 + 4          ○ 7 = 3 + 4

## Spiral Review (CC.K.CC.5, CC.K.CC.3)

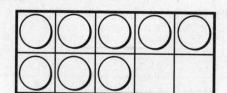

○          ○          ○          ○

**3**

four          five          six          seven

○          ○          ○          ○

**DIRECTIONS  1.** Which addition sentence shows a pair of numbers that matches the cube train? Mark beside your answer. **(Lesson 5.9)   2.** How many more counters would you place to model a way to make 10? Mark under your answer. **(Lesson 4.1)   3.** Count and tell how many hats. Mark under your answer. **(Lesson 3.4)**

**P98** ninety-eight

Name _____

# Algebra • Number Pairs for 8

**COMMON CORE STANDARD** CC.K.OA.3
Understand addition as putting together and adding to, and understand subtraction as taking apart and taking from.

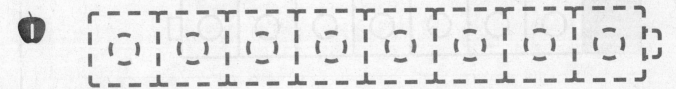

**1** 8 = _____ + _____

**2** 8 = _____ + _____

**3** 8 = _____ + _____

**4** 8 = _____ + _____

**DIRECTIONS** Use two colors of cubes to make a cube train to show the number pairs that make 8. **1–4.** Complete the addition sentence to show a number pair for 8. Color the cube train to match the addition sentence in Exercise 4.

© Houghton Mifflin Harcourt Publishing Company

## Lesson Check (CC.K.OA.3)

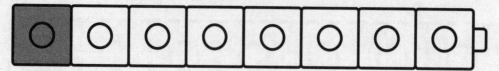

○ 8 = 1 + 7          ○ 9 = 1 + 8

○ 8 = 6 + 2          ○ 9 = 7 + 2

## Spiral Review (CC.K.CC.6, CC.K.OA.3)

2                3                4                5

○                ○                ○                ○

○                ○                ○                ○

**DIRECTIONS   1.** Which addition sentence shows a pair of numbers that matches the cube train? Mark beside your answer. **(Lesson 5.10)   2.** Mark under the number that is greater than the number of counters. **(Lesson 2.2)   3.** How many more counters would you place in the five frame to show a way to make 5? Mark under your answer. **(Lesson 1.7)**

Name _____

# Algebra • Number Pairs for 9

COMMON CORE STANDARD CC.K.OA.3
Understand addition as putting together
and adding to, and understand subtraction
as taking apart and taking from.

**1**

  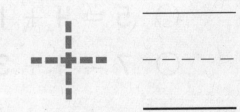

**2**

    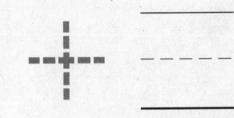

**3**

    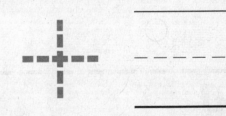

**4**

  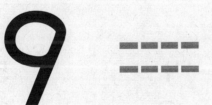  

**DIRECTIONS** Use two colors of cubes to make a cube train to show the number pairs that make 9. **1–4.** Complete the addition sentence to show a number pair for 9. Color the cube train to match the addition sentence in Exercise 4.

Chapter 5

## Lesson Check (CC.K.OA.3)

**1**

○ $5 = 4 + 1$        ○ $8 = 5 + 3$

○ $7 = 4 + 3$        ○ $9 = 5 + 4$

## Spiral Review (CC.K.CC.3, CC.K.CC.6)

| 8 | 7 | 6 | 5 |
|---|---|---|---|
| ○ | ○ | ○ | ○ |

**3**

| 2 | 3 | 4 | 5 |
|---|---|---|---|
| ○ | ○ | ○ | ○ |

**DIRECTIONS** 1. Which addition sentence shows a pair of numbers that matches the cube train? Mark beside your answer. **(Lesson 5.11)** 2. Count how many birds. Mark under your answer. **(Lesson 3.6)** 3. Mark under the number that is less than the number of counters. **(Lesson 2.3)**

Name _____

# Algebra • Number Pairs for 10

**COMMON CORE STANDARD** CC.K.OA.3
Understand addition as putting together and adding to, and understand subtraction as taking apart and taking from.

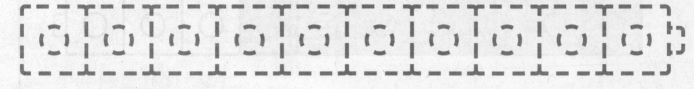

❶ $10 = \underline{\hspace{3cm}} + \underline{\hspace{3cm}}$

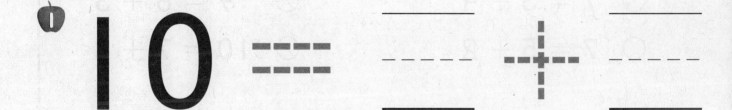

❷ $10 = \underline{\hspace{3cm}} + \underline{\hspace{3cm}}$

❸ $10 = \underline{\hspace{3cm}} + \underline{\hspace{3cm}}$

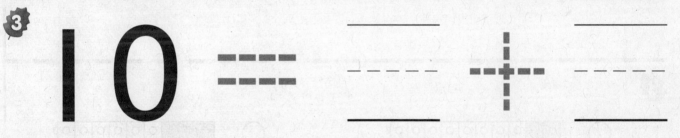

❹ $10 = \underline{\hspace{3cm}} + \underline{\hspace{3cm}}$

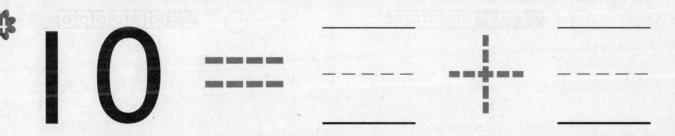

**DIRECTIONS** Use two colors of cubes to build a cube train to show the number pairs that make 10. **1–4.** Complete the addition sentence to show a number pair for 10. Color the cube train to match the addition sentence in Exercise 4.

## Lesson Check (CC.K.OA.3)

○ 7 = 3 + 4          ○ 9 = 6 + 3

○ 7 = 5 + 2          ○ 10 = 7 + 3

## Spiral Review (CC.K.CC.4c, CC.K.OA.4)

○ 5, 3, 4, 1, 2          ○ 1, 2, 4, 5, 3

○ 1, 2, 3, 4, 5          ○ 3, 5, 1, 2, 4

○          ○

○          ○

**DIRECTIONS** 1. Which addition sentence shows a pair of numbers that matches the cube train? Mark beside your answer. (Lesson 5.12)  2. Which set of numbers is in order? Mark beside your answer. (Lesson 1.8)  3. Which cube train shows a way to make 10? Mark beside your answer. (Lesson 4.3)

COMMON CORE STANDARDS CC.K.OA.1, CC.K.OA.2, CC.K.OA.3, CC.K.OA.4, CC.K.OA.5

# Chapter 5 Extra Practice

## Lessons 5.1 - 5.3 (pp. 169–180) • • • • • • • • • • • • • • • • • • •

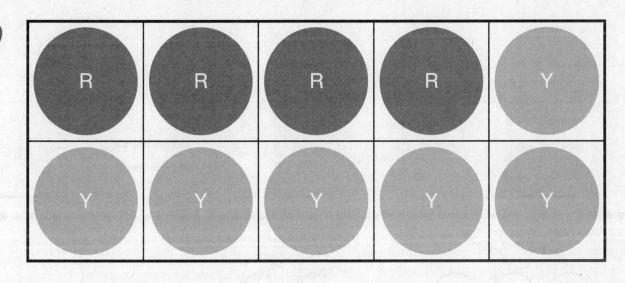

_____

- - -

_____ **and** _____

- - -

_____

  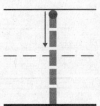 

**DIRECTIONS** 1. Place counters in the ten frame as shown. R is for red, and Y is for yellow. How many of each color counter? Write the numbers. 2. Tell an addition word problem about the puppies. Trace the numbers and the symbols. Write the number that shows how many puppies there are now.

# Lesson 5.4 - 5.12 (pp. 181-216)

**1**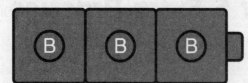

$$3 + 1 = \_\_\_$$

---

**2**

$$\_\_\_ + 2 = 7$$

---

**3**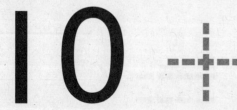

$$10 + \_\_\_ = \_\_\_$$

**DIRECTIONS** **1.** Place cubes as shown. B is for blue, and Y is for yellow. Tell an addition word problem. Model to show the cubes put together. Draw the cube train. Trace and write to complete the addition sentence. **2.** Tell an addition word problem. Circle the set being added. Write and trace to complete the addition sentence. **3.** Use two colors of cubes to build a cube train to show a number pair that makes 10. Complete the addition sentence to show a number pair for 10. Color the cube train to match the addition sentence.

# School-Home Letter

## Dear Family,

My class started Chapter 6 this week. In this chapter, I will learn how to show subtraction.

Love, _____

### Vocabulary

**minus (−)** a symbol that shows subtraction

minus
↓
3 − 2 = 1

**subtract** to take apart or take from

### Home Activity

Invite your child to act out subtraction word problems. For example, your child can show you five spoons, take away two spoons, and then tell you the subtraction sentence.

5 − 2 = 3

### Literature

Look for these books at the library. You and your child will enjoy these books that strengthen subtraction skills.

**Elevator Magic** by Stuart J. Murphy. HarperCollins, 1997.

**Ten Red Apples** by Pat Hutchins. Greenwillow Books, 2000.

# Carta
## para la casa

## Querida familia:

Mi clase comenzó el Capítulo 6 esta semana. En este capítulo aprenderé cómo mostrar una resta.

Con cariño, _____

## Vocabulario

**menos (−)** signo que indica una resta

**signo de resta**

$$3 - 2 = 1$$

**restar** quitar

## Actividad para la casa

Anime a su hijo para que represente problemas de resta. Por ejemplo, su hijo puede mostrarle 5 cucharas, quitar 2 cucharas y luego decirle el enunciado de la resta.

$$5 - 2 = 3$$

## Literatura

Busque este libro en una biblioteca. Su hijo y usted disfrutarán de este libro interactivo que fortalecerá las destrezas para restar.

**Elevator Magic** por Stuart J. Murphy. HarperTrophy, 1997.

**Ten Red Apples** por Pat Hutchins. Greenwillow Books, 2000.

# Subtraction: Take From

**COMMON CORE STANDARD** CC.K.OA.1
Understand addition as putting together and adding to, and understand subtraction as taking apart and taking from.

_____

- - - - -

_____      **take away**      _____

- - - - -

_____

_____

- - - - -

_____

---

**DIRECTIONS  I.** Tell a subtraction word problem about the children. Write the number that shows how many children in all. Write the number that shows how many children are leaving. Write the number that shows how many children are left.

## Lesson Check (CC.K.OA.1)

# 3 take away 1

| 1 | 2 | 3 | 4 |
|:-:|:-:|:-:|:-:|
| ○ | ○ | ○ | ○ |

## Spiral Review (CC.K.CC.5, CC.K.OA.2)

| 2 | 3 | 4 | 5 |
|:-:|:-:|:-:|:-:|
| ○ | ○ | ○ | ○ |

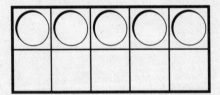

| ○ | ○ | ○ | ○ |
|:-:|:-:|:-:|:-:|

**DIRECTIONS    1.** Which number shows how many frogs are left? Mark under your answer. **(Lesson 6.1)    2.** Which number completes the addition sentence about the sets of birds? Mark under your answer. **(Lesson 5.7)    3.** How many more counters would you place to model a way to make 8? Mark under your answer. **(Lesson 3.5)**

Name _____

# Subtraction: Take Apart

**COMMON CORE STANDARD** CC.K.OA.1
Understand addition as putting together
and adding to, and understand subtraction
as taking apart and taking from.

**1**

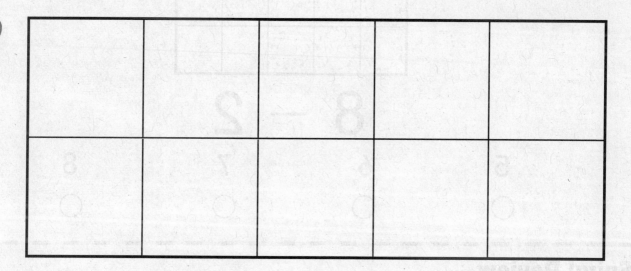

9    minus    3

_____          _____

‑ ‑ ‑ ‑      ▬▬▬      ‑ ‑ ‑ ‑

_____          _____

_____

‑ ‑ ‑ ‑ ‑

_____

---

**DIRECTIONS  1.** Listen to the subtraction word problem. Jane has
nine counters. Three of her counters are red. The rest of her counters
are yellow. How many are yellow? Place nine counters in the ten
frame. Draw and color the counters. Write the number that shows
how many in all. Write the number that shows how many are red.
Write the number that shows how many are yellow.

## Lesson Check (CC.K.OA.1)

**1**

$$8 - 2$$

| 5 | 6 | 7 | 8 |
|---|---|---|---|
| ○ | ○ | ○ | ○ |

## Spiral Review (CC.K.CC.6)

**2**

| 2 | 3 | 4 | 5 |
|---|---|---|---|
| ○ | ○ | ○ | ○ |

**3**

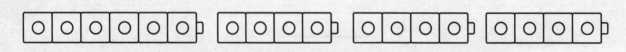

| ○ | ○ | ○ | ○ |
|---|---|---|---|

**DIRECTIONS** **1.** Clyde has eight counters. Two of his counters are yellow. The rest of his counters are red. How many are red? Mark under your answer. **(Lesson 6.2)** **2.** Mark under the number that is greater than the number of objects. **(Lesson 2.5)** **3.** Compare the cube trains. Mark under the cube train that has a greater number of cubes. **(Lesson 4.5)**

Name _____

# Problem Solving • Act Out Subtraction Problems

**COMMON CORE STANDARD** CC.K.OA.1
Understand addition as putting together and adding to, and understand subtraction as taking apart and taking from.

 --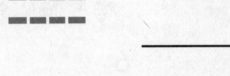

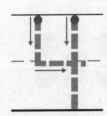 --

**DIRECTIONS** **1.** Tell a subtraction word problem about the beavers. Trace the numbers and the symbols. Write the number that shows how many beavers are left. **2.** Draw to show what you know about the subtraction sentence. Write how many are left. Tell a friend about your drawing.

## Lesson Check (CC.K.OA.1)

**1**

$$5 - 4 = \underline{\quad}$$

| 1 | 2 | 3 | 4 |
|:-:|:-:|:-:|:-:|
| ○ | ○ | ○ | ○ |

---

## Spiral Review (CC.K.CC.3, CC.K.CC.5)

**2**

| 6 | 7 | 8 | 9 |
|:-:|:-:|:-:|:-:|
| ○ | ○ | ○ | ○ |

---

**3**

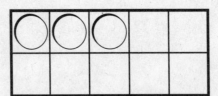

| ○ | ○ | ○ | ○ |
|:-:|:-:|:-:|:-:|

---

**DIRECTIONS** **1.** Which number shows how many birds are left? Mark under your answer. **(Lesson 6.3)** **2.** Count and tell how many bees. Mark under your answer. **(Lesson 3.8)** **3.** How many more counters would you place to model a way to make 7? Mark under your answer. **(Lesson 3.3)**

**P114** one hundred fourteen

Name _____

# Algebra • Model and Draw Subtraction Problems

COMMON CORE STANDARD CC.K.OA.5
Understand addition as putting together
and adding to, and understand subtraction
as taking apart and taking from.

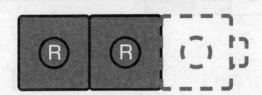

 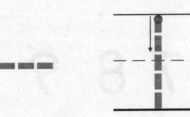

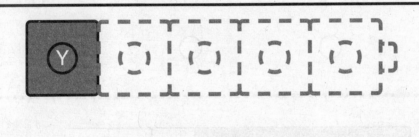

 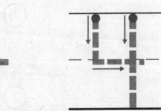 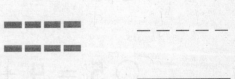

**DIRECTIONS** **1.** Model a three-cube train. Two cubes are red and the rest are blue.
Take apart the cube train to show how many cubes are blue. Draw and color the cube trains.
Trace and write to complete the subtraction sentence. **2.** Model a five-cube train. One cube
is yellow and the rest are green. Take apart the train to show how many cubes are green.
Draw and color the cube trains. Trace and write to complete the subtraction sentence.

## Lesson Check (CC.K.OA.5)

**1**

○ 5 − 1 = 4        ○ 4 − 3 = 1

○ 5 − 2 = 3        ○ 4 − 2 = 2

## Spiral Review (CC.K.CC.2, CC.K.OA.3)

**2**

# 5 ___ 7 8 9 10

3                4                5                6

○                ○                ○                ○

**3**

○ 5 = 3 + 2        ○ 8 = 5 + 3

○ 5 = 4 + 1        ○ 8 = 6 + 2

**DIRECTIONS   1.** Ellie makes the cube train shown. She takes the cube train apart to show how many cubes are gray. Mark beside the subtraction sentence that shows Ellie's cube train. **(Lesson 6.4)   2.** Begin with 5. Count forward. Mark under the number that fills the space. **(Lesson 4.4)   3.** Which addition sentence shows a pair of numbers that matches the cube train? Mark beside your answer. **(Lesson 5.10)**

# Algebra • Write Subtraction Sentences

COMMON CORE STANDARD CC.K.OA.5
Understand addition as putting together and adding to, and understand subtraction as taking apart and taking from.

**1**

4 – 3 = ____

**2**

3 – 1 = ____

**3**

5 – 4 = ____

**DIRECTIONS** 1–3. Listen to the subtraction word problem about the animals. There are _____ _____. Some are taken from the set. Now there are _____. How many were taken from the set? Circle and mark an X to show how many are being taken from the set. Trace and write to complete the subtraction sentence.

## Lesson Check (CC.K.OA.5)

**1**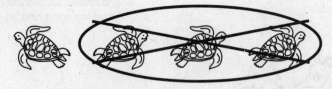

$$4 - \underline{\quad} = 1$$

| 1 | 2 | 3 | 4 |
|:-:|:-:|:-:|:-:|
| ○ | ○ | ○ | ○ |

## Spiral Review (CC.K.CC.5, CC.K.CC.6)

**2**

| 1 | 2 | 3 | 4 |
|:-:|:-:|:-:|:-:|
| ○ | ○ | ○ | ○ |

**3**

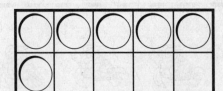

           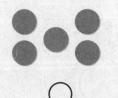

| ○ | ○ | ○ | ○ |
|:-:|:-:|:-:|:-:|

**DIRECTIONS  1.** Mark under the number to show how many are being taken from the set. **(Lesson 6.5)  2.** Mark under the number that is greater than the number of counters. **(Lesson 2.2)  3.** How many more counters would you place to model a way to make 9? Mark under your answer. **(Lesson 3.7)**

P118  one hundred eighteen

# Algebra • Write More Subtraction Sentences

COMMON CORE STANDARD CC.K.OA.2
Understand addition as putting together and adding to, and understand subtraction as taking apart and taking from.

  **1**

_____  _ _ _  =  **4**  =  **3**

_____

---

  **2**

_____  _ _ _  **3**  =  **6**

_____

---

  **3**

_____  _ _ _  **1**  =  **5**

_____

---

**DIRECTIONS** 1–3. Listen to a subtraction word problem about the birds. There are some birds. _____ birds are taken from the set. Draw more birds to show how many you started with. How many birds did you start with? Write the number to complete the subtraction sentence.

## Lesson Check (CC.K.OA.2)

**1**

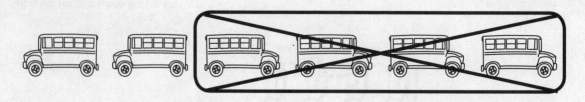

$$\underline{\hspace{1.5cm}} - 4 = 2$$

| 5 | 6 | 7 | 8 |
|---|---|---|---|
| ○ | ○ | ○ | ○ |

## Spiral Review (CC.K.CC.3, CC.K.CC.4c)

**2**

| 4 | 5 | 6 | 7 |
|---|---|---|---|
| ○ | ○ | ○ | ○ |

**3**

○ 1, 2, 3, 4, 5          ○ 2, 4, 3, 5, 1

○ 1, 3, 4, 2, 5          ○ 3, 2, 1, 4, 5

**DIRECTIONS   1.** Mark under the number that would complete the subtraction sentence. **(Lesson 6.6)   2.** How many lunch boxes are there? Mark under your answer. **(Lesson 3.4)   3.** Which set of numbers is in order? Mark beside your answer. **(Lesson 1.8)**

# Algebra • Addition and Subtraction

**COMMON CORE STANDARD** CC.K.OA.2
Understand addition as putting together and adding to, and understand subtraction as taking apart and taking from.

_____   +   _____   ===   _____

_____   ---   _____   ===   _____

**DIRECTIONS  1–2.** Tell an addition or subtraction word problem.
Use cubes to add or subtract. Complete the number sentence.

## Lesson Check (CC.K.OA.2)

1.

○ 3 + 5 = 8          ○ 8 − 3 = 5

○ 5 + 3 = 8          ○ 8 − 5 = 3

## Spiral Review (CC.K.CC.7, CC.K.OA.3)

2.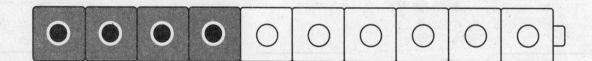

○ 10 = 7 + 3         ○ 8 = 6 + 2

○ 10 = 4 + 6         ○ 8 = 5 + 3

3.

# 8

7          I          9          5

○          ○          ○          ○

---

**DIRECTIONS** 1. Mark beside the number sentence that matches the picture. **(Lesson 6.7)**
2. Which addition sentence shows a pair of numbers that matches the cube train? Mark beside your answer. **(Lesson 5.12)** 3. Which number is greater than 8? Mark under your answer. **(Lesson 4.7)**

# Chapter 6 Extra Practice

## Lessons 6.1 - 6.2 (pp. 225–232) • • • • • • • • • • • • • • • • • • • •

_____    _____

—————    —————

_____   **take away**   _____

— — — —

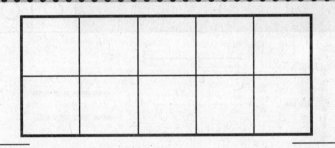

_____          _____

— — — —   ▬ ▬ ▬   — — — —

_____          _____

— — — —

_____

**DIRECTIONS   1.** Tell a subtraction word problem about the children. Write the number that shows how many children in all. Write the number that shows how many children are leaving. Write the number that shows how many children are left.   **2.** Listen to the subtraction word problem. Jamal has eight counters. Two of his counters are yellow. The rest of his counters are red. How many counters are red? Draw and color eight counters in the ten frame. Write the number that shows how many in all. Write the number that shows how many are yellow. Write the number that shows how many are red.

# Lessons 6.3 – 6.7 (pp. 233–252)

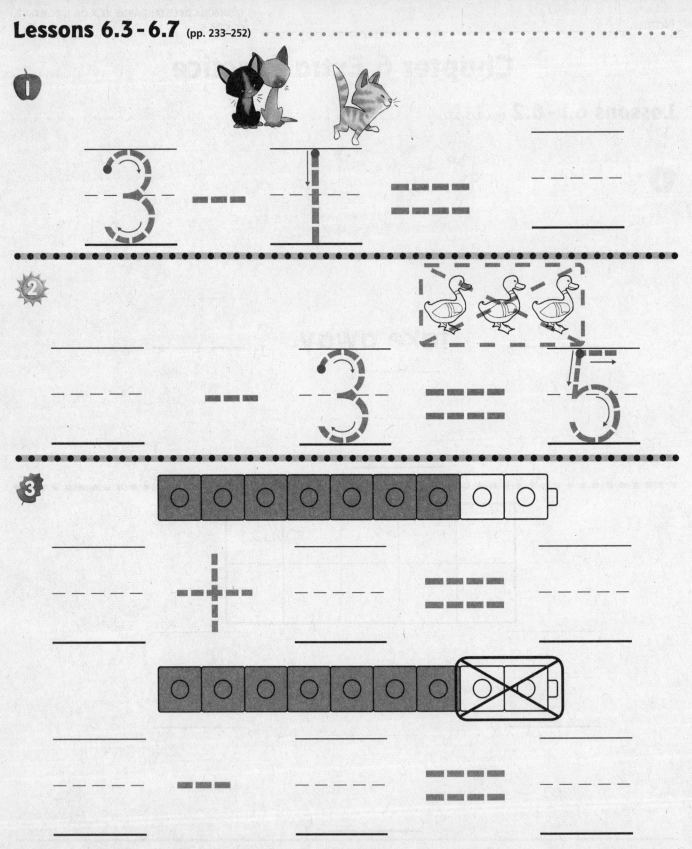

**1.**  $3 - 1 =$ _____

**2.**  _____ $- 3 =$ 5

**3.**  _____ $+$ _____ $=$ _____

_____ $-$ _____ $=$ _____

**DIRECTIONS**  **1.** Tell a subtraction word problem about the kittens. Trace the numbers and the symbols. Write the number that shows how many kittens are left.  **2.** Tell a subtraction word problem about the ducks. Draw more ducks to show how many you started with. Write the number to complete the subtraction sentence.  **3.** Tell addition and subtraction word problems. Use cubes to add and subtract. Complete the number sentences.

# School-Home Letter

## Dear Family,

My class started Chapter 7 this week. In this chapter, I will learn how to show, count, and write numbers 11 to 19.

Love, _____

## Vocabulary

**eleven** 10 ones and 1 one

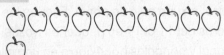

**sixteen** 10 ones and 6 ones

**nineteen** 10 ones and 9 ones

## Home Activity

Draw a ten frame on a sheet of paper. Write numbers 11 to 19 on small pieces of paper and place them face down in a pile. Have your child turn over the cards and use small objects, such as pennies, to model the numbers.

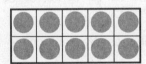

## Literature

Look for this book at the library. You and your child will have fun looking at the pages while building your child's counting skills.

**Bears at the Beach: Counting 10 to 20** by Niki Yektai. Millbrook Press, 2001.

# Carta
### para la casa

## Querida familia:

Mi clase comenzó el Capítulo 7 esta semana. En este capítulo, aprenderé cómo mostrar, contar y escribir los números del 11 al 19.

Con cariño, _____

## Vocabulario

**once** uno más que diez

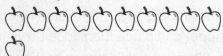

**dieciséis** uno más que quince

**diecinueve** uno más que dieciocho

## Actividad para la casa

Dibuje dos cuadros de diez, uno al lado del otro, en una hoja de papel. Escriba los números del 11 al 19 en pequeños trozos de papel y póngalos boca abajo en una pila. Pídale a su hijo que dé vuelta las cartas y que use objetos pequeños como monedas de 1 ¢ para representar los números.

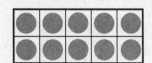

12

## Literatura

Busque estos libros en la biblioteca. Usted y su hijo se divertirán mirando las páginas mientras refuerzan las destrezas de contar.

**Bears at the Beach: Counting 10 to 20** por Niki Yektai. Millbrook Press, 2001.

## Model and Count 11 and 12

**COMMON CORE STANDARD CC.K.NBT.1**
Work with numbers 11–19 to gain
foundations for place value.

**1 2**
**twelve**

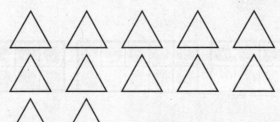

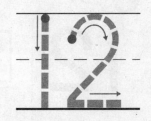

**2**

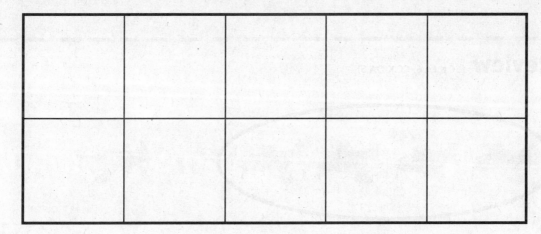

**3**

 _____ **ones and** _____ **ones**

**DIRECTIONS   1.** Count and tell how many. Trace the number. **2.** Use counters to show
the number 12. Draw the counters. **3.** Look at the counters you drew. How many ones are
in the ten frame? Trace the number. How many more ones are there? Write the number.

## Lesson Check (CC.K.NBT.1)

 **12**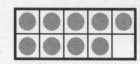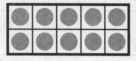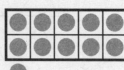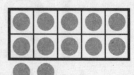

 ○    ○   ○    ○

---

## Spiral Review (CC.K.CC.6, CC.K.OA.5)

$$4 + \underline{\hspace{1cm}} = 5$$

1           2           3           4
○           ○           ○           ○

---

2           3           4           5
○           ○           ○           ○

---

**DIRECTIONS**   **1.** Which set of counters shows the number 12? Mark under your answer. (Lesson 7.1)
**2.** Which number completes the addition sentence about the sets of airplanes? Mark under your
answer. (Lesson 5.6)   **3.** Mark under the number that is less than the number of counters. (Lesson 2.3)

# Count and Write 11 and 12

COMMON CORE STANDARD CC.K.CC.3
Know number names and the
count sequence.

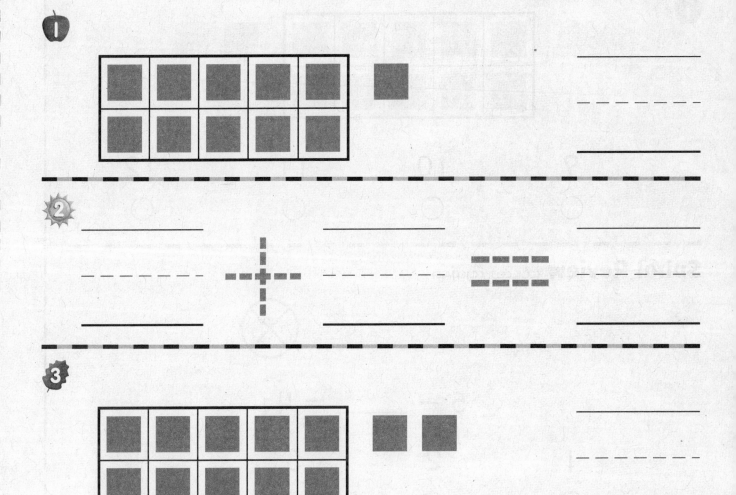

**1** _____

_ _ _ _ _ _ _ _ _ _ _

_____

**2** _ _ _ _ _ _ _ _   +   _ _ _ _ _ _ _ _   = ▬ ▬ ▬ ▬
_____     _____   ▬ ▬ ▬ ▬

**3** _____

_ _ _ _ _ _ _ _ _ _ _

_____

**4** _____   +   _____   = ▬ ▬ ▬
_ _ _ _ _ _ _ _       _ _ _ _ _ _ _ _     ▬ ▬ ▬
_____       _____

**DIRECTIONS   1.** Count and tell how many. Write the number.
**2.** Look at the ten ones and some more ones in Exercise 1.
Complete the addition sentence to match. **3.** Count and tell how
many. Write the number. **4.** Look at the ten ones and some more
ones in Exercise 3. Complete the addition sentence to match.

## Lesson Check (CC.K.CC.3)

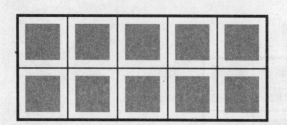

| 9 | 10 | 11 | 12 |
|---|----|----|----|
| ◯ | ◯ | ◯ | ◯ |

## Spiral Review (CC.K.CC.3, CC.K.OA.5)

$$5 - \underline{\quad} = 4$$

| 1 | 2 | 3 | 4 |
|---|---|---|---|
| ◯ | ◯ | ◯ | ◯ |

| 6 | 5 | 4 | 3 |
|---|---|---|---|
| ◯ | ◯ | ◯ | ◯ |

**DIRECTIONS** 1. How many tiles are there? Mark under your answer. (Lesson 7.2)
2. Mark under the number to show how many are being taken from the set. (Lesson 6.5)
3. How many birds are there? Mark under your answer. (Lesson 3.2)

Name _____

# Model and Count 13 and 14

**COMMON CORE STANDARD** CC.K.NBT.1
Work with numbers 11–19 to gain
foundations for place value.

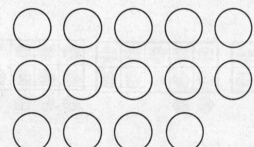

**14**
fourteen

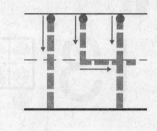

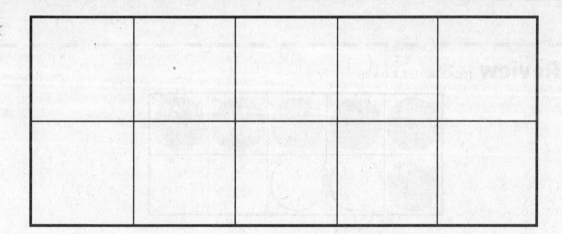

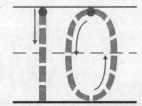

_____ ones and _____ ones

**DIRECTIONS** 1. Count and tell how many. Trace the number. 2. Use counters to show the number 14. Draw the counters. 3. Look at the counters you drew. How many ones are in the ten frame? Trace the number. How many more ones are there? Write the number.

## Lesson Check (CC.K.NBT.1)

 **13** |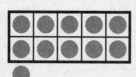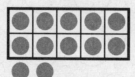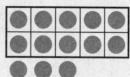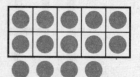

○   ○   ○   ○

## Spiral Review (CC.K.OA.1, CC.K.OA.2)

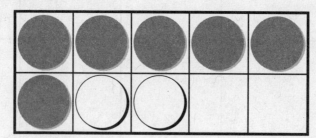

3 + 2     4 + 4     5 + 1     6 + 2

○         ○         ○         ○

____ − 1 = 5

5         6         7         8

○         ○         ○         ○

**DIRECTIONS** 1. Which set of counters shows the number 13? Mark under your answer. (Lesson 7.3)
2. Look at the counters in the ten frame. Which pair of numbers shows the sets of counters? Mark under your answer. (Lesson 5.2) 3. Mark under the number that would complete the subtraction sentence. (Lesson 6.6)

Name _____

# Count and Write 13 and 14

COMMON CORE STANDARD CC.K.CC.3
Know number names and the count sequence.

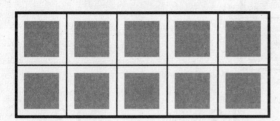 

_____

_ _ _ _ _ _ _ _

_____

_____   _____

_ _ _ _ _ _ _    _ _ _ _ _ _ _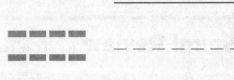

_____   _____

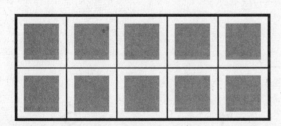  

_____

_ _ _ _ _ _ _ _

_____

_____   _____

_ _ _ _ _ _ _    _ _ _ _ _ _ _

_____   _____

**DIRECTIONS** 1. Count and tell how many. Write the number.
2. Look at the ten ones and some more ones in Exercise 1.
Complete the addition sentence to match. 3. Count and tell how
many. Write the number. 4. Look at the ten ones and some more
ones in Exercise 3. Complete the addition sentence to match.

**1**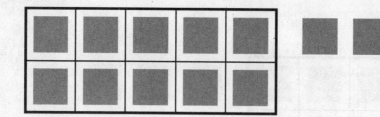

10          11          12          13

○          ○          ○          ○

**Spiral Review** (CC.K.CC.4c, CC.K.OA.1)

**2**

$$3 - 1 = \underline{\hspace{1cm}}$$

2                3                4                5

○                ○                ○                ○

**3**

| 5, 4, 1, 2, 3 | 1, 2, 3, 4, 5 | 3, 1, 4, 5, 2 | 1, 2, 5, 3, 4 |
| :-: | :-: | :-: | :-: |
| ○ | ○ | ○ | ○ |

**DIRECTIONS** **1.** How many tiles are there? Mark under your answer. (Lesson 7.4)   **2.** Which number shows how many kittens are left? Mark under your answer. (Lesson 6.3)   **3.** Which set of numbers is in order? Mark under your answer. (Lesson 1.8)

**P134** one hundred thirty-four

# Model, Count, and Write 15

COMMON CORE STANDARD CC.K.NBT.1
Work with numbers 11–19 to gain
foundations for place value.

 **1**

## 15
**fifteen**

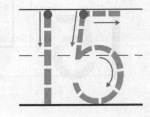

 **2**

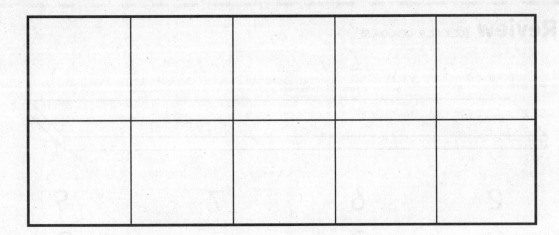

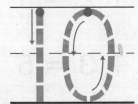 **3**

_____ **ones and** _____ **ones**

**DIRECTIONS   1.** Count and tell how many. Trace the number. **2.** Use counters to show the number 15. Draw the counters. **3.** Look at the counters you drew. How many ones are in the ten frame? Trace the number. How many more ones? Write the number.

## Lesson Check (CC.K.NBT.1)

# 15

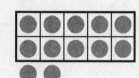 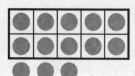 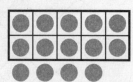 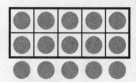

---

## Spiral Review (CC.K.CC.6, CC.K.OA.5)

2          6          7          9

○          ○          ○          ○

---

○  1 + 2 = 3          ○  2 + 2 = 4

○  1 + 3 = 4          ○  2 + 3 = 5

---

**DIRECTIONS** 1. Which set of counters shows the number 15? Mark under your answer. (Lesson 7.5)
2. Draw to solve this problem. The number of plates on the shelf is two less than 8. How many plates are on the shelf? Mark under your answer. (Lesson 3.9) 3. Which addition sentence shows the cubes being put together? Mark beside your answer. (Lesson 5.4)

**P136** one hundred thirty-six

## Problem Solving • Use Numbers to 15

**COMMON CORE STANDARD** CC.K.CC.3
Know number names and the count sequence.

_____
_____ **carrot plants**

**DIRECTIONS** There are 15 vegetables in the garden. They are planted in rows of 5. There are 2 carrot plants and 3 potato plants in each row. How many carrot plants are in the garden? Draw to solve the problem.

one hundred thirty-seven **P137**

## Lesson Check (CC.K.CC.3)

| 9 | 11 | 14 | 15 |
|---|----|----|----|
| ○ | ○  | ○  | ○  |

## Spiral Review (CC.K.OA.2, CC.K.OA.4)

$$\underline{\quad\quad} - 5 = 3$$

| 6 | 7 | 8 | 9 |
|---|---|---|---|
| ○ | ○ | ○ | ○ |

$$6 + \underline{\quad\quad} = 10$$

| 1 | 3 | 4 | 5 |
|---|---|---|---|
| ○ | ○ | ○ | ○ |

**DIRECTIONS** **1.** How many tiles are there? Mark under your answer. (Lesson 7.6) **2.** Mark under the number that would complete the subtraction sentence. (Lesson 6.6) **3.** Mark under the number that makes 10 when put together with the given number. (Lesson 5.5)

**HANDS ON**
Lesson 7.7

# Model and Count 16 and 17

COMMON CORE STANDARD CC.K.NBT.1
Work with numbers 11–19 to gain
foundations for place value.

**1** 

17
**seventeen**

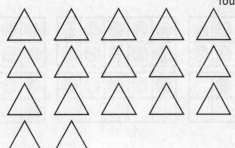

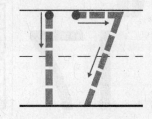

**2**

**3**

 _____ **ones and** _____ **ones**

**DIRECTIONS**  **1.** Count and tell how many. Trace the number.  **2.** Place counters in the ten frames to show the number 17. Draw the counters.  **3.** Look at the counters you drew in the ten frames. How many ones are in the top ten frame? Trace the number. How many ones are in the bottom ten frame? Write the number.

# Lesson Check (CC.K.NBT.1)

**1**

# 17

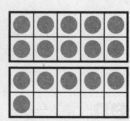

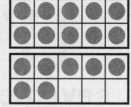

○        ○        ○        ○

# Spiral Review (CC.K.CC.4b, CC.K.OA.1)

**2**

$$2 + 1 = \underline{\hphantom{00}}$$

| 1 | 2 | 3 | 4 |
|---|---|---|---|
| ○ | ○ | ○ | ○ |

**3**

# 5

○        ○        ○        ○

---

**DIRECTIONS  1.** Which set of counters shows the number 17?
Mark under your answer. **(Lesson 7.7)  2.** How many puppies are there
in all? Mark under your answer. **(Lesson 5.3)  3.** Which set shows the
number? Mark under your answer. **(Lesson 1.6)**

**P140**  one hundred forty

Name _____

# Count and Write 16 and 17

COMMON CORE STANDARD CC.K.CC.3
Know number names and the
count sequence.

**1**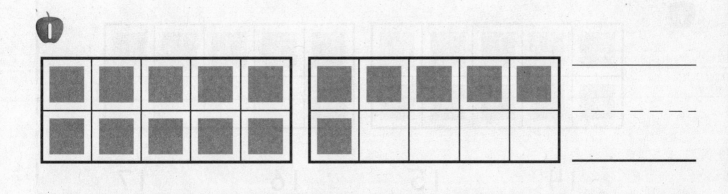

**2**

**3**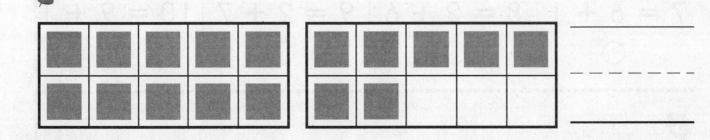

**4**

**DIRECTIONS** **1.** Count and tell how many. Write the number. **2.** Look at the ten frames in Exercise 1. Complete the addition sentence to match. **3.** Count and tell how many. Write the number. **4.** Look at the ten frames in Exercise 3. Complete the addition sentence to match.

## Lesson Check (CC.K.CC.3)

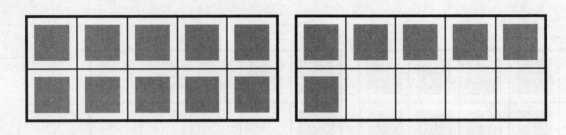

| 14 | 15 | 16 | 17 |
|:--:|:--:|:--:|:--:|
| ○ | ○ | ○ | ○ |

## Spiral Review (CC.K.CC.3, CC.K.OA.3)

| $7 = 6 + 1$ | $8 = 2 + 6$ | $9 = 2 + 7$ | $10 = 9 + 1$ |
|:--:|:--:|:--:|:--:|
| ○ | ○ | ○ | ○ |

| 1 | 2 | 3 | 4 |
|:--:|:--:|:--:|:--:|
| ○ | ○ | ○ | ○ |

**DIRECTIONS**  **1.** How many tiles are there? Mark under your answer.  (Lesson 7.8)
**2.** Which addition sentence shows a number pair that matches the cube train? Mark under your answer.  (Lesson 5.11)  **3.** How many bicycles are there? Mark under your answer.  (Lesson 1.2)

# Model and Count 18 and 19

**COMMON CORE STANDARD** CC.K.NBT.1
Work with numbers 11–19 to gain
foundations for place value.

**1**

# 19
## nineteen

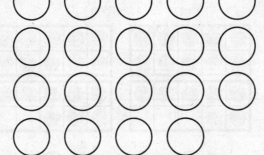

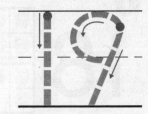

**2**

**3**

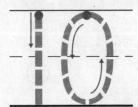 **ones and** _____ **ones**

**DIRECTIONS** **1.** Count and tell how many. Trace the number. **2.** Place counters in the ten frame to show the number 19. Draw the counters. **3.** Look at the counters you drew in the ten frames. How many ones are in the top ten frame? Trace the number. How many ones are in the bottom ten frame? write the numbers.

**Chapter 7**

one hundred forty-three **P143**

© Houghton Mifflin Harcourt Publishing Company

# Lesson Check (CC.K.NBT.1)

**18**

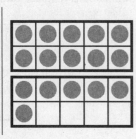 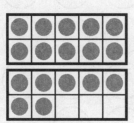 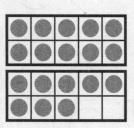 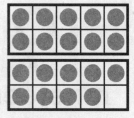

○        ○        ○        ○

# Spiral Review (CC.K.OA.1, CC.K.OA.3)

○ $8 = 4 + 4$        ○ $10 = 5 + 5$

○ $8 = 7 + 1$        ○ $10 = 9 + 1$

## 4 take away 2

1        2        6        7

○        ○        ○        ○

**DIRECTIONS 1.** Which set of counters shows the number 18? Mark under your answer. **(Lesson 7.9) 2.** Which addition sentence shows a number pair that matches the cube train? Mark under your answer. **(Lesson 5.12) 3.** Which number shows how many birds are left? Mark under your answer. **(Lesson 6.1)**

Name _____

# Count and Write 18 and 19

COMMON CORE STANDARD CC.K.CC.3
Know number names and the count sequence.

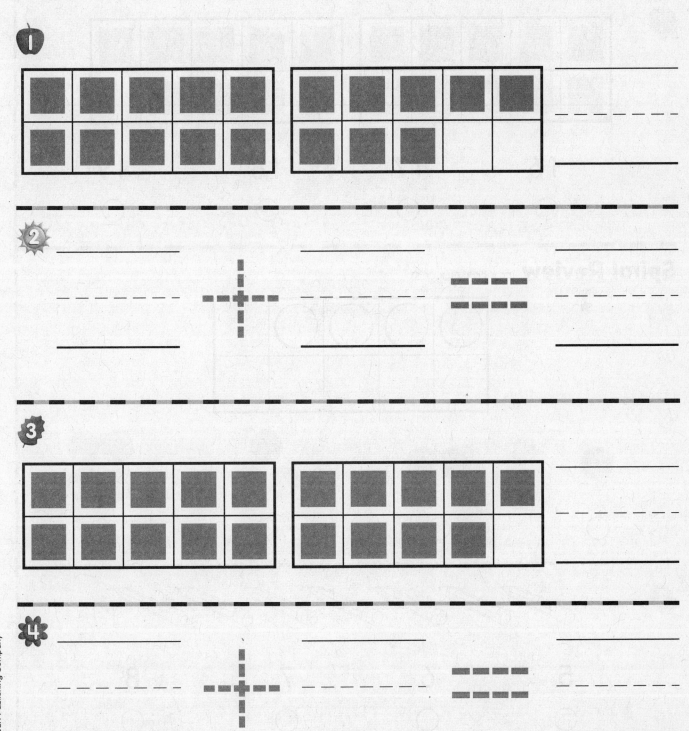

**1**

**2**

**3**

**4**

**DIRECTIONS** **1.** Count and tell how many. Write the number. **2.** Look at the ten frames in Exercise 1. Complete the addition sentence to match. **3.** Count and tell how many. Write the number. **4.** Look at the ten frames in Exercise 3. Complete the addition sentence to match.

**Chapter 7**

## Lesson Check (CC.K.CC.3)

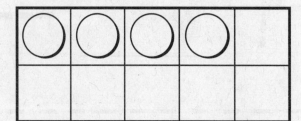

16        17        18        19
○         ○         ○         ○

## Spiral Review (CC.K.CC.3, CC.K.CC.5)

○         ○         ○         ○

 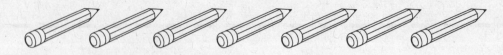

5        6        7        8
○        ○        ○        ○

**DIRECTIONS** 1. How many tiles are there? Mark under your answer. (Lesson 7.10)
2. How many more counters would you place to model a way to make 8?
Mark under your answer. (Lesson 3.5)  3. How many pencils are there? Mark under
your answer. (Lesson 3.4)

Name _____

# Chapter 7 Extra Practice

## Lessons 7.1-7.5 (pp. 261–280) · · · · · · · · · · · · · · · · · · · · · · ·

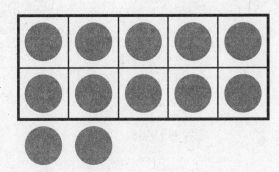

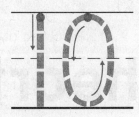 _____ _____ ones and _____ ones

· · · · · · · · · · · · · · · · · · · · · · · · · · · · · · · · · · · · · · · · · · · · · ·

  _____
_____
_____

· · · · · · · · · · · · · · · · · · · · · · · · · · · · · · · · · · · · · · · · · · · · · ·

_____   +   _____   =   _____

---

**DIRECTIONS** 1. Look at the counters. How many ones are in the ten frame? Trace the number. How many more ones are there? Write the number. 2. Count and tell how many. Write the number. 3. Look at the ten ones and some more ones in Exercise 2. Complete the addition sentence to match.

**①**

_____

_____ **hearts**

**②**

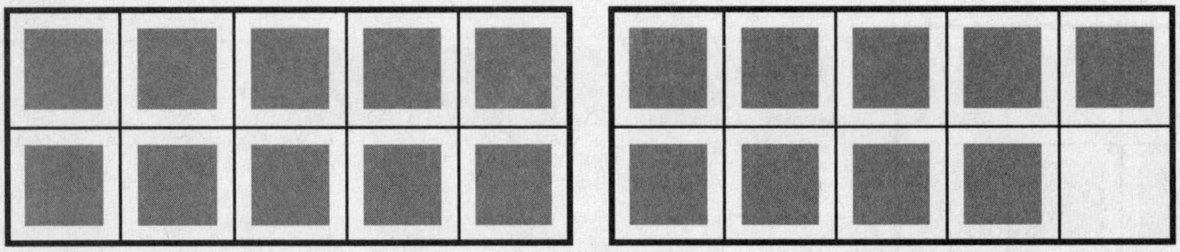

_____

_____

**③**

_____ **+** _____ **=** _____

**DIRECTIONS** **1.** Maya has 15 stickers. She places them on a page in rows of 5. There are 2 flowers and 3 hearts in each row. How many hearts are on the page? Draw to solve the problem. Write how many hearts are on the page. **2.** Count and tell how many. Write the number. **3.** Look at the ten frames in Exercise 2. Complete the addition sentence to match.

# School-Home Letter

## Dear Family,

My class started Chapter 8 this week. In this chapter, I will learn how to show, count, and write numbers to 20 and beyond.

Love, _____

## Vocabulary

**twenty** 1 ten and 10 ones

20

## Home Activity

Make a set of number flash cards. Ask your child to lay out 20 cards to model what a set of 20 objects looks like. Then ask your child to place the number cards in the correct order from 1 to 20. Have your child point to each card and count forward from the number 1.

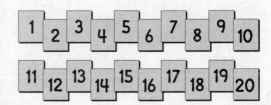

## Literature

Look for these books at the library. Your child will enjoy these fun books while continuing to build counting skills.

**20 Hungry Piggies** by Trudy Harris. Millbrook Press, 2006.

**Count!** by Denise Fleming. Henry Holt and Co., 1995.

# Carta
## para la casa

## Querida familia:

Mi clase comenzó el Capítulo 8 esta semana. En este capítulo, aprenderé cómo mostrar, contar y escribir números hasta el 20 y más allá. .

Con cariño, _____

## Vocabulario

**veinte** una decena y 10 unidades

20

## Actividad para la casa

Tome un conjunto de tarjetas nemotécnicas con números. Pídale a su hijo que separe 20 tarjetas para mostrar cómo es un conjunto de 20. Luego, pídale que ponga las tarjetas en el orden correcto del 1 al 20. Pídale a su hijo que señale cada carta y que cuente hacia delante desde el número 1.

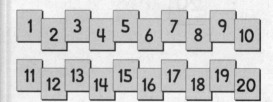

## Literatura

Busque estos libros en la biblioteca. Su hijo disfrutará de estos libros divertidos mientras continua construir las habilidades de recuento.

**20 Hungry Piggies** por Trudy Harris. Millbrook Press, 2006.

**Count!** por Denise Fleming. Henry Holt and Co., 1995.

# Model and Count 20

**COMMON CORE STANDARD** CC.K.CC.5
Count to tell the number of objects.

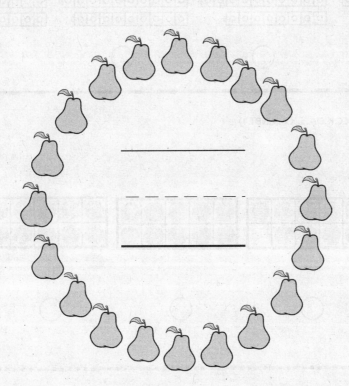

_____
- - - - - - -
_____

_____
- - - - - - -
_____

**DIRECTIONS** 1–2. Count and tell how many pieces of fruit. Write the number. Tell a friend how you counted the fruit.

## Lesson Check (CC.K.CC.5)

 1

○    ○    ○    ○

---

## Spiral Review (CC.K.OA.5, CC.K.NBT.1)

 2

11 |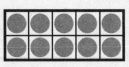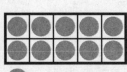

○    ○    ○    ○

---

 3

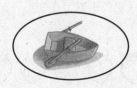

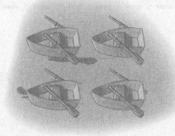

$$1 \ + \ \underline{\qquad} \ = \ 5$$

2      3      4      5

○    ○    ○    ○

---

**DIRECTIONS** 1. Which set of cubes models the number 20? Mark under your answer. **(Lesson 8.1)** 2. Which set of counters shows the number 11? Mark under your answer. **(Lesson 7.1)** 3. Which number completes the addition sentence about the sets of boats? Mark under your answer. **(Lesson 5.6)**

# Count and Write 20

COMMON CORE STANDARD CC.K.CC.3
Know number names and the
count sequence.

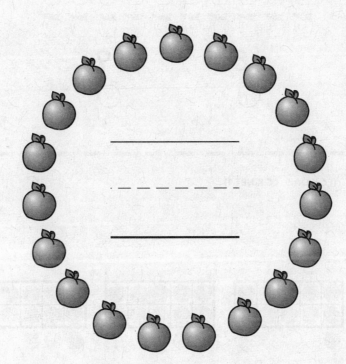

_____

- - - - - - - - - - - - -

_____

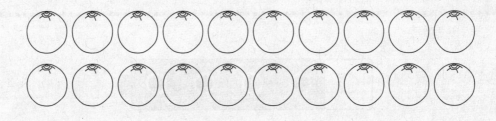

_____

- - - - - - - - - - - - -

_____

**DIRECTIONS** 1–2. Count and tell how many pieces of fruit. Write
the number.

## Lesson Check (CC.K.CC.3)

**1**

17       18       19       20

○       ○       ○       ○

## Spiral Review (CC.K.OA.5, CC.K.NBT.1)

**2**

14    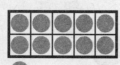    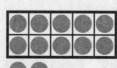       

○       ○       ○       ○

**3**

○   $1 + 3 = 4$      ○   $2 + 1 = 3$

○   $1 + 4 = 5$      ○   $2 + 2 = 4$

**DIRECTIONS** 1. Count and tell how many pieces of fruit. Mark under your answer. (Lesson 8.2) 2. Which set of counters shows the number 14? Mark under your answer. (Lesson 7.3) 3. Which addition sentence shows the cubes being put together? Mark beside your answer. (Lesson 5.4)

# Count and Order to 20

COMMON CORE STANDARD CC.K.CC.2
Know number names and the count sequence.

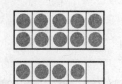 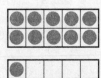   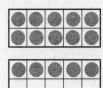

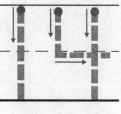

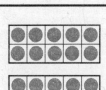 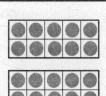 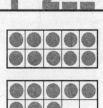 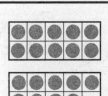

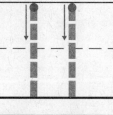

**DIRECTIONS** 1. Count the dots in each set of ten frames. Trace or write the numbers. 2. Trace and write those numbers in order.

## Lesson Check (CC.K.CC.2)

○ 14, 16, 13, 15     ○ 13, 14, 15, 16

○ 15, 13, 16, 14     ○ 16, 14, 15, 13

## Spiral Review (CC.K.CC.3, CC.K.OA.2)

_____ + 4 = 7

    1        2        3        4

    ○        ○        ○        ○

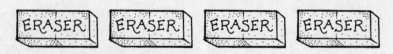

    4        3        2        1

    ○        ○        ○        ○

**DIRECTIONS** **1.** Which set of numbers is in order? Mark beside your answer. **(Lesson 8.3)** **2.** Which number completes the addition sentence about the sets of cats? Mark under your answer. **(Lesson 5.7)** **3.** How many erasers are there? Mark under your answer. **(Lesson 1.4)**

# Problem Solving • Compare
# Numbers to 20

COMMON CORE STANDARD CC.K.CC.6
Compare numbers.

**1**
_____

_ _ _ _ _ _ _

_____

_ _ _ _ _ _ _

_____

**2**
_____

_ _ _ _ _ _ _

_____

_____

_ _ _ _ _ _ _

_____

**DIRECTIONS    1.** Teni has 16 berries. She has a number of berries two greater than Marta. Use cubes to model the sets of berries. Compare the sets. Which set is larger? Draw the cubes. Write how many in each set. Circle the greater number. Tell a friend how you compared the numbers.    **2.** Ben has 18 pears. Sophia has a number of pears two less than Ben. Use cubes to model the sets of pears. Compare the sets. Which set is smaller? Draw the cubes. Write how many in each set. Circle the number that is less. Tell a friend how you compared the numbers.

# Lesson Check (CC.K.CC.6)

◯        ◯        ◯        ◯

# Spiral Review (CC.K.CC.6, CC.K.NBT.1)

   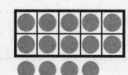   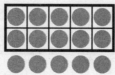   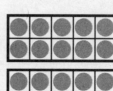   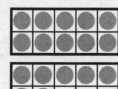

◯        ◯        ◯        ◯

1        2        3        4

◯        ◯        ◯        ◯

**DIRECTIONS** **1.** Compare the sets. Which set has a number of cubes two less than 20? Mark under your answer. **(Lesson 8.4)** **2.** Which set of counters shows the number 16? Mark under your answer. **(Lesson 7.7)** **3.** Mark under the number that is greater than the number of counters. **(Lesson 2.2)**

**P158** one hundred fifty-eight

# Count to 50 by Ones

COMMON CORE STANDARD CC.K.CC.1
Know number names and the
count sequence.

| 1 | 2 | 3 | 4 | 5 | 6 | 7 | 8 | 9 | 10 |
|---|---|---|---|---|---|---|---|---|---|
| 11 | 12 | 13 | 14 | 15 | 16 | 17 | 18 | 19 | 20 |
| 21 | 22 | 23 | 24 | 25 | 26 | 27 | 28 | 29 | 30 |
| 31 | 32 | 33 | 34 | 35 | 36 | 37 | 38 | 39 | 40 |
| 41 | 42 | 43 | 44 | 45 | 46 | 47 | 48 | 49 | 50 |

**DIRECTIONS** 1. Look away and point to any number. Circle that number. Count forward from that number. Draw a line under the number 50.

## Lesson Check (CC.K.CC.1)

| 1 | 2 | 3 | 4 | 5 | 6 | 7 | 8 | 9 | 10 |
|---|---|---|---|---|---|---|---|---|----|
| 11 | 12 | 13 | 14 | 15 | 16 | 17 | 18 | 19 | 20 |
| 21 | 22 | 23 | 24 | 25 | 26 | 27 | 28 | 29 | 30 |

| 20 | 21 | 22 | 23 |
|----|----|----|----|
| ○ | ○ | ○ | ○ |

## Spiral Review (CC.K.OA.1, CC.K.OA.3)

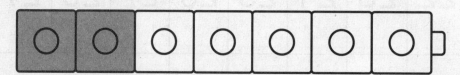

| $6 = 5 + 1$ | $5 = 2 + 3$ | $6 = 2 + 4$ | $7 = 2 + 5$ |
|----|----|----|----|
| ○ | ○ | ○ | ○ |

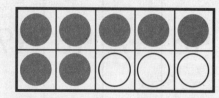 $10 - 3$

| 5 | 6 | 7 | 8 |
|---|---|---|---|
| ○ | ○ | ○ | ○ |

**DIRECTIONS** **1.** Begin with 1 and count forward to 20. What is the next number? Mark under your answer. **(Lesson 8.5)** **2.** Which addition sentence shows a numbers pair that matches the cube train? Mark under your answer. **(Lesson 5.9)** **3.** Shelley has 10 counters. Three of her counters are white. The rest of her counters are gray. How many are gray? Mark under your answer. **(Lesson 6.2)**

Name _____

# Count to 100 by Ones

COMMON CORE STANDARD CC.K.CC.1
Know number names and the
count sequence.

| 1 | 2 | 3 | 4 | 5 | 6 | 7 | 8 | 9 | 10 |
|---|---|---|---|---|---|---|---|---|---|
| 11 | 12 | 13 | 14 | 15 | 16 | 17 | 18 | 19 | 20 |
| 21 | 22 | 23 | 24 | 25 | 26 | 27 | 28 | 29 | 30 |
| 31 | 32 | 33 | 34 | 35 | 36 | 37 | 38 | 39 | 40 |
| 41 | 42 | 43 | 44 | 45 | 46 | 47 | 48 | 49 | 50 |
| 51 | 52 | 53 | 54 | 55 | 56 | 57 | 58 | 59 | 60 |
| 61 | 62 | 63 | 64 | 65 | 66 | 67 | 68 | 69 | 70 |
| 71 | 72 | 73 | 74 | 75 | 76 | 77 | 78 | 79 | 80 |
| 81 | 82 | 83 | 84 | 85 | 86 | 87 | 88 | 89 | 90 |
| 91 | 92 | 93 | 94 | 95 | 96 | 97 | 98 | 99 | 100 |

**DIRECTIONS** 1. Point to each number as you count to 100. Look away and point to any number. Circle that number. Count forward to 100 from that number. Draw a line under the number 100.

## Lesson Check (CC.K.CC.1)

**1**

| 71 | 72 | 73 | 74 | 75 | 76 | 77 | 78 | 79 | 80 |
|----|----|----|----|----|----|----|----|----|-----|
| 81 | 82 | 83 | 84 | 85 | 86 | 87 | 88 | 89 | 90 |
| 91 | 92 | 93 | 94 | 95 | 96 | 97 | 98 | 99 | 100 |

   80      81      82      90

   ○      ○      ○      ○

## Spiral Review (CC.K.CC.6, CC.K.OA.5)

**2**

$3 - 1 = 2$ | $3 - 2 = 1$ | $4 - 2 = 2$ | $4 - 3 = 1$

  ○       ○       ○       ○

**3**

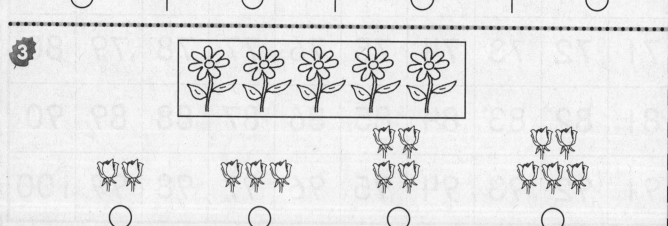

  ○       ○       ○       ○

**DIRECTIONS** **1.** Begin with 71 and count forward to 80. What is the next number? Mark under your answer. **(Lesson 8.6)** **2.** Pete makes the cube train shown. He takes the cube train apart to show how many cubes are gray. Mark under the subtraction sentence that shows Pete's cube train. **(Lesson 6.4)** **3.** Which set shows the number of roses is the same as the number of daisies? **(Lesson 2.1)**

# Count to 100 by Tens

COMMON CORE STANDARD CC.K.CC.1
Know number names and the
count sequence.

| 51 | 52 | 53 | 54 | 55 | 56 | 57 | 58 | 59 | 60 |
| 61 | 62 | 63 | 64 | 65 | 66 | 67 | 68 | 69 | 70 |
| 71 | 72 | 73 | 74 | 75 | 76 | 77 | 78 | 79 | 80 |
| 81 | 82 | 83 | 84 | 85 | 86 | 87 | 88 | 89 | 90 |
| 91 | 92 | 93 | 94 | 95 | 96 | 97 | 98 | 99 | 100 |

**DIRECTIONS** 1. Trace the numbers to complete the counting order to 100. Count by tens as you point to the numbers you traced.

## Lesson Check (CC.K.CC.1)

**1**

| 1 | 2 | 3 | 4 | 5 | 6 | 7 | 8 | 9 | 10 |
|---|---|---|---|---|---|---|---|---|---|
| 11 | 12 | 13 | 14 | 15 | 16 | 17 | 18 | 19 | 20 |
| 21 | 22 | 23 | 24 | 25 | 26 | 27 | 28 | 29 | 30 |

17          20          23          30
○            ○            ○            ○

## Spiral Review (CC.K.CC.3, CC.K.OA.5)

**2**

11          12          13          14
○            ○            ○            ○

**3**

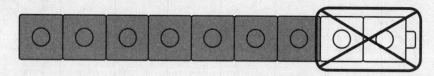

2 + 7 = 9 | 7 + 2 = 9 | 9 − 2 = 7 | 9 − 7 = 2
○                 ○                 ○                 ○

---

**DIRECTIONS** **1.** Count by tens as you point to the numbers in the shaded boxes. Start with the number 10. What number do you end with? Mark under your answer. **(Lesson 8.7)**
**2.** How many tiles are there? Mark under your answer. **(Lesson 7.4)** **3.** Mark under the number sentence that matches the picture. **(Lesson 6.7)**

**P164** one hundred sixty-four

Name _____

# Count by Tens

COMMON CORE STANDARD CC.K.CC.1
Know number names and the
count sequence.

**1**

**20**　　**30**　　**40**

**2**

**30**　　**40**　　**50**

**3**

**60**　　**70**　　**80**

**4**

**80**　　**90**　　**100**

**5**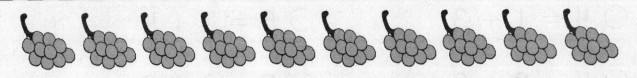

**80**　　**90**　　**100**

**DIRECTIONS** 1–5. Point to each set of 10 as you count by tens.
Circle the number that shows how many.

## Lesson Check (CC.K.CC.1)

 ❶

| 60 | 70 | 80 | 90 |
|----|----|----|----|
| ○ | ○ | ○ | ○ |

## Spiral Review (CC.K.OA.3, CC.K.NBT.1)

❷

# 15

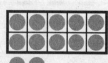   

    ○      ○      ○      ○

 ❸

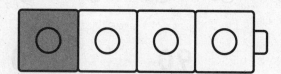

○ 4 = 1 + 3        ○ 5 = 1 + 4

○ 4 = 2 + 2        ○ 5 = 2 + 3

**DIRECTIONS  1.** Point to each set of 10 as you count by tens. Mark under the number that shows how many crayons there are. **(Lesson 8.8) 2.** Which set of counters shows the number 15? Mark under your answer. **(Lesson 7.5) 3.** Which addition sentence shows a number pair that matches the cube train? Mark beside your answer. **(Lesson 5.8)**

# Chapter 8 Extra Practice

## Lessons 8.1 – 8.4 (pp. 309–323) · · · · · · · · · · · · · · · · · ·

_____

_ _ _ _ _ _ _ _ _ _ _ _

 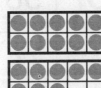 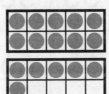 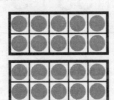 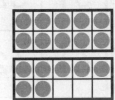

_____ _____ _____ _____ _____

_____ _____ _____ _____ _____

_____ _____ _____ _____ _____

_____ _____ _____ _____ _____

 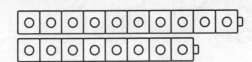

_____              _____

_ _ _ _              _ _ _ _

_____              _____

**DIRECTIONS   1.** Count and tell how many pieces of fruit. Write the number.   **2.** Count the dots in the ten frames. Write the numbers.   **3.** Look at the numbers you wrote in Exercise 2. Trace and write those numbers in order.   **4.** Gina has 18 cubes. She has a number of cubes one greater than Oscar. Compare the sets of cubes. Which set is larger? Write how many in each set. Circle the greater number.

| 31 | 32 | 33 | 34 | 35 | 36 | 37 | 38 | 39 | 40 |
|----|----|----|----|----|----|----|----|----|----|
| 41 | 42 | 43 | 44 | 45 | 46 | 47 | 48 | 49 | 50 |
| 51 | 52 | 53 | 54 | 55 | 56 | 57 | 58 | 59 | 60 |
| 61 | 62 | 63 | 64 | 65 | 66 | 67 | 68 | 69 | 70 |
| 71 | 72 | 73 | 74 | 75 | 76 | 77 | 78 | 79 | 80 |
| 81 | 82 | 83 | 84 | 85 | 86 | 87 | 88 | 89 | 90 |
| 91 | 92 | 93 | 94 | 95 | 96 | 97 | 98 | 99 | 100 |

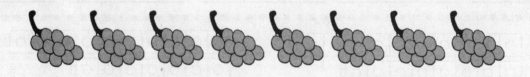

**80**　　　　**90**　　　　**100**

**DIRECTIONS  1.** Point to each number as you count forward from 31 to 50. Draw a line under the number 50. Point to each number as you count forward from 50 to 100. Circle the number 100. Color the boxes of all the numbers that end with a zero. Count by tens as you point to the numbers in the boxes you colored. **2.** Point to each set of 10 as you count by tens. Circle the number that shows how many.

# School-Home Letter

## Dear Family,

My class started Chapter 9 this week. In this chapter, I will learn how to identify, name, and describe two-dimensional shapes.

Love, _____

## Vocabulary

**curve** a line that is rounded

**vertex** the point where two sides of a two-dimensional shape meet

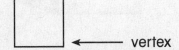
← vertex

## Home Activity

Spread out a group of household objects. Have your child point out the objects that look like circles, squares, and triangles.

## Literature

Look for these books at the library. The pictures will capture your child's imagination.

**Shapes, Shapes, Shapes** by Tana Hoban. Greenwillow, 1996.

**Color Farm** by Lois Ehlert. HarperCollins, 1990.

# Carta
## para la casa

## Querida familia:

Mi clase comenzó el Capítulo 9 esta semana. En este capítulo, aprenderé cómo identi car, nombrar y describir  guras bidimensionales.

Con cariño, _____

## Vocabulario

**curva** una línea que no es recta

**vértice** el punto en donde se encuentran dos lados de una figura bidimensional

← vértice

## Actividad para la casa

Dé a su hijo varios objetos que encuentre en la casa y pídale que señale los que se parezcan a los cuadrados, círculos y triángulos.

## Literatura

Busque este libro en la biblioteca. Las ilustraciones estimularán la imaginación de su hijo.

**Shapes, Shapes, Shapes**
por Tana Hoban.
Greenwillow, 1996.

**Color Farm**
por Lois Ehlert.
HarperCollins, 1990.

Name _____

# Identify and Name Circles

COMMON CORE STANDARD CC.K.G.2
Identify and describe shapes (squares, circles, triangles, rectangles, hexagons, cubes, cones, cylinders, and spheres).

**1**

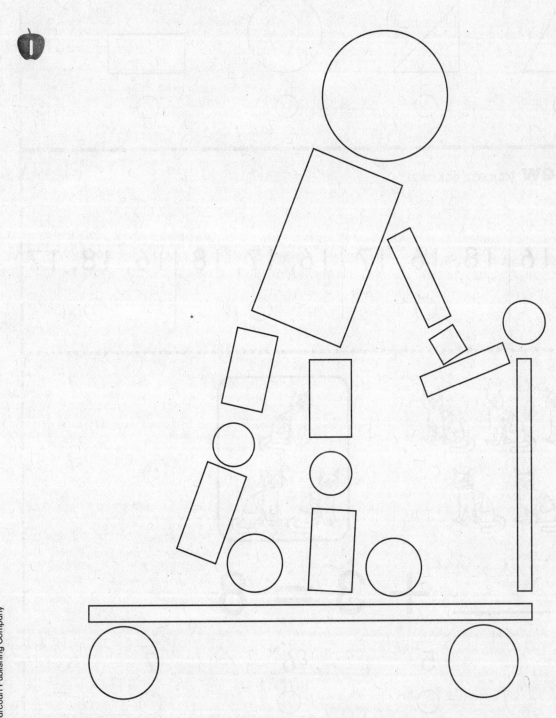

---

**DIRECTIONS** **1.** Color the circles in the picture.

**Chapter 9**

## Lesson Check (CC.K.G.2)

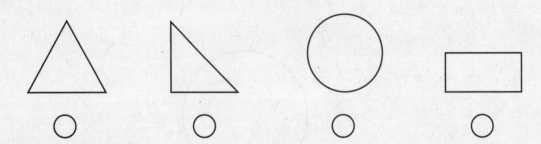

○      ○      ○      ○

## Spiral Review (CC.K.CC.2, CC.K.OA.2)

17, 18, 16 | 18, 16, 17 | 16, 17, 18 | 16, 18, 17

○      ○      ○      ○

___ + 3 = 8

4           5           6           7

○           ○           ○           ○

**DIRECTIONS   1.** Which shape is a circle? Mark under your answer.
**(Lesson 9.1)   2.** Which set of numbers is in order? Mark under your
answer.  **(Lesson 8.3)   3.** Which number completes the addition sentence
about the sets of cats? Mark under your answer.  **(Lesson 5.7)**

# Describe Circles

**COMMON CORE STANDARD** CC.K.G.4
Analyze, compare, create, and
compose shapes.

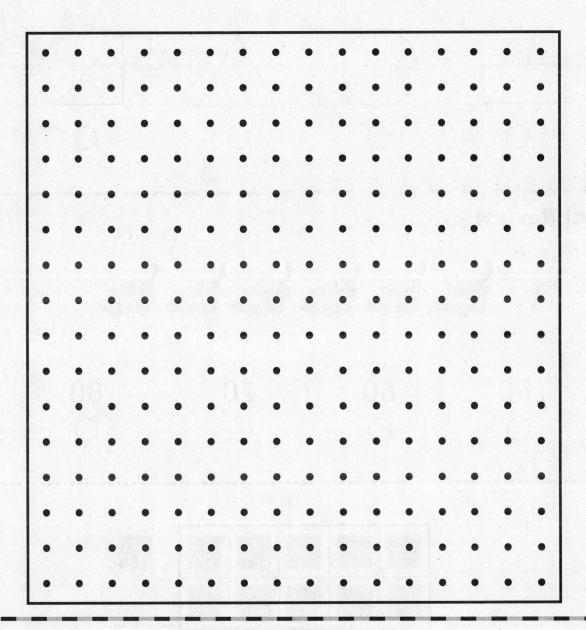

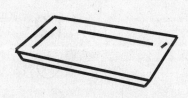 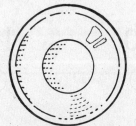 

**DIRECTIONS** **1.** Use a pencil to hold one end of a large paper clip on one of the dots in the center. Place another pencil in the other end of the paper clip. Move the pencil around to draw a circle. **2.** Color the object that is shaped like a circle.

# Lesson Check (CC.K.G.4)

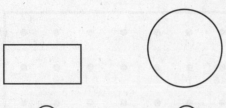  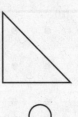

○          ○          ○          ○

# Spiral Review (CC.K.CC.1, CC.K.CC.3)

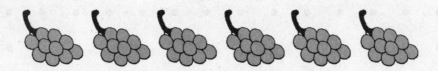

| 50 | 60 | 70 | 80 |

○          ○          ○          ○

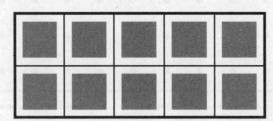

| 9 | 10 | 11 | 12 |

○          ○          ○          ○

---

**DIRECTIONS** **1.** Which shape has a curve? Mark under your answer.
**(Lesson 9.2)** **2.** Point to each set of 10 as you count by tens. Mark under the
number that shows how many grapes there are. **(Lesson 8.8)** **3.** How many
tiles are there? Mark under your answer. **(Lesson 7.2)**

Name _____

# Identify and Name Squares

COMMON CORE STANDARD CC.K.G.2
Identify and describe shapes (squares, circles, triangles, rectangles, hexagons, cubes, cones, cylinders, and spheres).

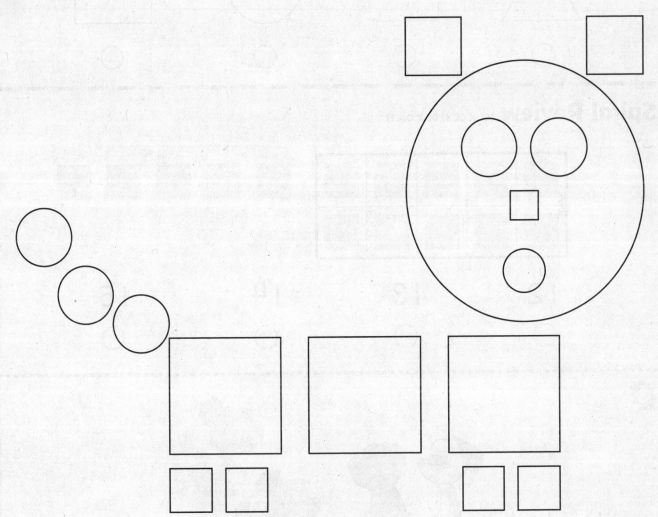

---

**DIRECTIONS**  1. Color the squares in the picture.

**Chapter 9**

one hundred seventy-five  **P175**

## Lesson Check (CC.K.G.2)

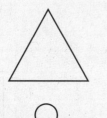    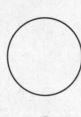  

○          ○          ○          ○

## Spiral Review (CC.K.CC.3, CC.K.OA.1)

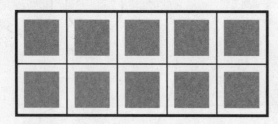

12          13          14          15

○          ○          ○          ○

2          3          4          5

○          ○          ○          ○

**DIRECTIONS**  1. Which shape is a square? Mark under your answer.
(Lesson 9.3)  2. How many tiles are there? Mark under your answer.  (Lesson 7.6)
3. How many puppies are there in all? Mark under your answer.  (Lesson 5.3)

**P176**  one hundred seventy-six

Name _____

# Describe Squares

COMMON CORE STANDARD CC.K.G.4
Analyze, compare, create, and compose shapes.

**1**

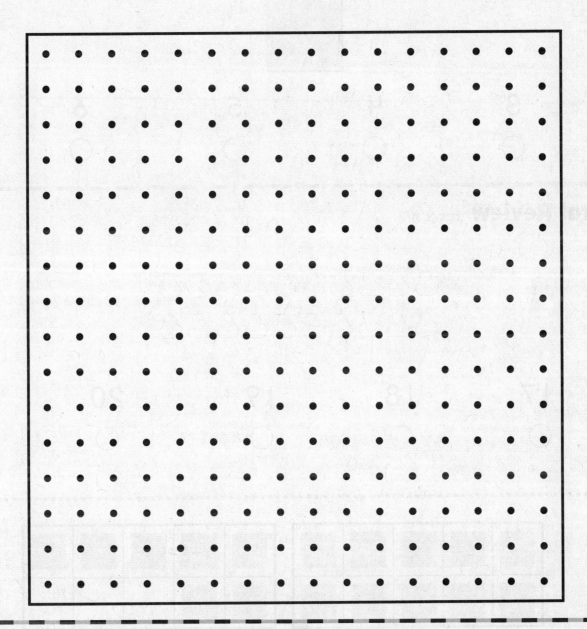

**2** _____ vertices ⋮ **3** _____ sides

**DIRECTIONS** 1. Draw and color a square. 2. Place a counter on each corner, or vertex, of the square that you drew. Write how many corners, or vertices. 3. Trace around the sides of the square that you drew. Write how many sides.

## Lesson Check (CC.K.G.4)

 **1**

3        4       5       6

○       ○       ○       ○

## Spiral Review (CC.K.CC.3)

 **2**

🍐🍐🍐🍐🍐🍐🍐🍐🍐🍐
🍐🍐🍐🍐🍐🍐🍐🍐🍐🍐

17      18      19      20

○       ○       ○       ○

 **3**

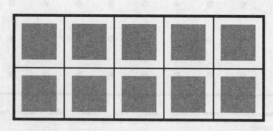

14      15      16      17

○       ○       ○       ○

**DIRECTIONS** **1.** How many vertices does the square have? Mark under your answer. **(Lesson 9.4)** **2.** Count and tell how many pieces of fruit. Mark under your answer. **(Lesson 8.2)** **3.** How many tiles are there? Mark under your answer. **(Lesson 7.8)**

# Identify and Name Triangles

COMMON CORE STANDARD CC.K.G.2
Identify and describe shapes (squares, circles, triangles, rectangles, hexagons, cubes, cones, cylinders, and spheres).

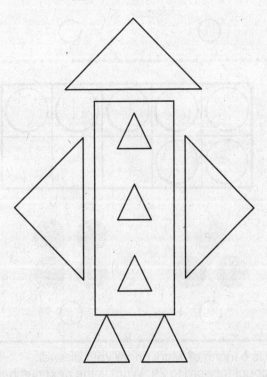

**DIRECTIONS** 1–2. Color the triangles in the picture.

## Lesson Check (CC.K.G.2)

 **1**

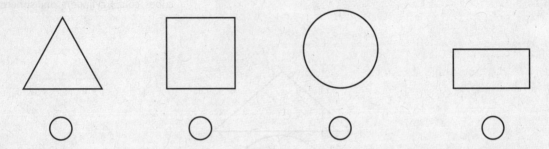

○          ○          ○          ○

## Spiral Review (CC.K.CC.1, CC.K.CC.5)

 **2**

| 1 | 2 | 3 | 4 | 5 | 6 | 7 | 8 | 9 | 10 |
|---|---|---|---|---|---|---|---|---|----|
| 11 | 12 | 13 | 14 | 15 | 16 | 17 | 18 | 19 | 20 |
| 21 | 22 | 23 | 24 | 25 | 26 | 27 | 28 | 29 | 30 |

24          25          26          27

○          ○          ○          ○

 **3**

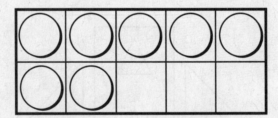

○          ○          ○          ○

**DIRECTIONS    1.** Which shape is a triangle? Mark under your answer.
**(Lesson 9.5)    2.** Begin with 1 and count forward to 24. What is the next number?
Mark under your answer. **(Lesson 8.5)    3.** How many more counters would you
place to model a way to make 10? Mark under your answer. **(Lesson 4.1)**

# Describe Triangles

COMMON CORE STANDARD CC.K.G.4
Analyze, compare, create, and
compose shapes.

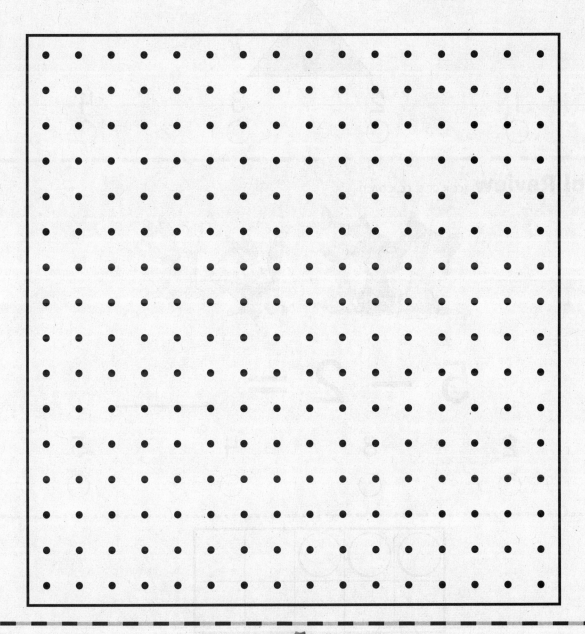

2  _____
   _ _ _ _ _

   _____ vertices

3  _____
   _ _ _ _ _

   _____ sides

**DIRECTIONS** 1. Draw and color a triangle.  2. Place a counter
on each corner, or vertex, of the triangle that you drew. Write how
many corners, or vertices.  3. Trace around the sides of the
triangle that you drew. Write how many sides.

## Lesson Check (CC.K.G.4)

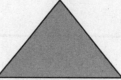

| 1 | 2 | 3 | 4 |
|---|---|---|---|
| ○ | ○ | ○ | ○ |

## Spiral Review (CC.K.CC.5, CC.K.OA.1)

$$5 - 2 = \underline{\hspace{2cm}}$$

| 2 | 3 | 4 | 5 |
|---|---|---|---|
| ○ | ○ | ○ | ○ |

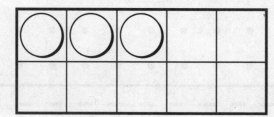

   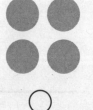

○      ○      ○      ○

**DIRECTIONS** **1.** How many sides does the triangle have? Mark under your answer. **(Lesson 9.6)** **2.** Which number shows how many kittens are left? Mark under your answer. **(Lesson 6.3)** **3.** How many more counters would you place to model a way to make 7? Mark under your answer. **(Lesson 3.3)**

Name _____

# Identify and Name Rectangles

**COMMON CORE STANDARD** CC.K.G.2
Identify and describe shapes (squares, circles, triangles, rectangles, hexagons, cubes, cones, cylinders, and spheres).

**DIRECTIONS** 1. Color the rectangles in the picture.

# Lesson Check (CC.K.G.2)

 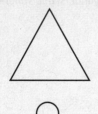 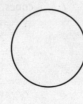 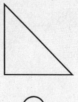 

◯          ◯          ◯          ◯

# Spiral Review (CC.K.CC.1, CC.K.CC.5)

| 1  | 2  | 3  | 4  | 5  | 6  | 7  | 8  | 9  | 10 |
|----|----|----|----|----|----|----|----|----|----|
| 11 | 12 | 13 | 14 | 15 | 16 | 17 | 18 | 19 | 20 |
| 21 | 22 | 23 | 24 | 25 | 26 | 27 | 28 | 29 | 30 |

10                15                27                30

◯          ◯          ◯          ◯

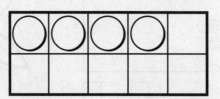

◯          ◯          ◯          ◯

**DIRECTIONS  1.** Which shape is a rectangle? Mark under your answer.
**(Lesson 9.7)  2.** Count by tens as you point to the numbers in the shaded boxes. Start with the number 10. What number do you end with? Mark under your answer. **(Lesson 8.7)  3.** How many more counters would you place to model a way to make 6? Mark under your answer. **(Lesson 3.1)**

# Describe Rectangles

COMMON CORE STANDARD CC.K.G.4

Analyze, compare, create, and compose shapes.

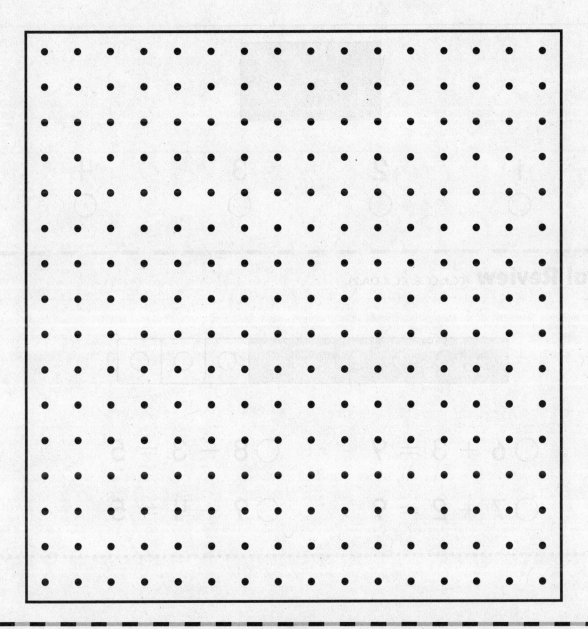

2 _____          3 _____

_____              _____

_____ **vertices** ┆ _____ **sides**

**DIRECTIONS** 1. Draw and color a rectangle. 2. Place a counter on each corner, or vertex, of the rectangle that you drew. Write how many corners, or vertices. 3. Trace around the sides of the rectangle that you drew. Write how many sides.

# Lesson Check (CC.K.G.4)

1    2    3    4
○    ○    ○    ○

# Spiral Review (CC.K.CC.6, CC.K.OA.2)

○ 6 + 3 = 9        ○ 8 − 3 = 5

○ 7 + 2 = 9        ○ 9 − 4 = 5

○        ○        ○        ○

**DIRECTIONS** 1. How many sides does the rectangle have? Mark under your answer. **(Lesson 9.8)** 2. Mark beside the number sentence that matches the picture. **(Lesson 6.7)** 3. Compare the sets. Which set has a number of cubes two greater than 18? Mark under your answer. **(Lesson 8.4)**

# Identify and Name Hexagons

COMMON CORE STANDARD CC.K.G.2
Identify and describe shapes (squares, circles, triangles, rectangles, hexagons, cubes, cones, cylinders, and spheres)

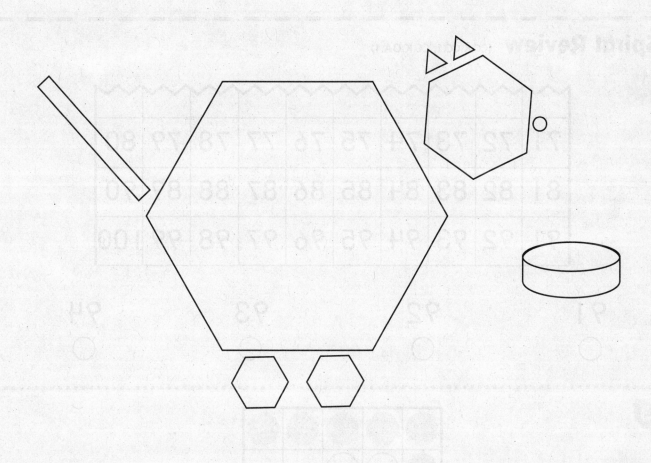

---

**DIRECTIONS** 1. Color the hexagons in the picture.

## Lesson Check (CC.K.G.2)

○        ○        ○        ○

---

## Spiral Review (CC.K.CC.1, CC.K.OA.1)

| 71 | 72 | 73 | 74 | 75 | 76 | 77 | 78 | 79 | 80 |
| 81 | 82 | 83 | 84 | 85 | 86 | 87 | 88 | 89 | 90 |
| 91 | 92 | 93 | 94 | 95 | 96 | 97 | 98 | 99 | 100 |

91          92          93          94
○           ○           ○           ○

---

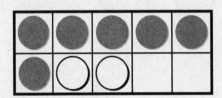

5 + 1        6 + 2        7 + 3        8 + 1
○           ○           ○           ○

---

**DIRECTIONS** **1.** Which shape is a hexagon? Mark under your answer.
**(Lesson 9.9)** **2.** Begin with 81 and count forward to 90. What is the next number? Mark under your answer. **(Lesson 8.6)** **3.** Which numbers show the sets that are put together? Mark under your answer. **(Lesson 5.2)**

# Describe Hexagons

**COMMON CORE STANDARD** CC.K.G.4
Analyze, compare, create, and
compose shapes.

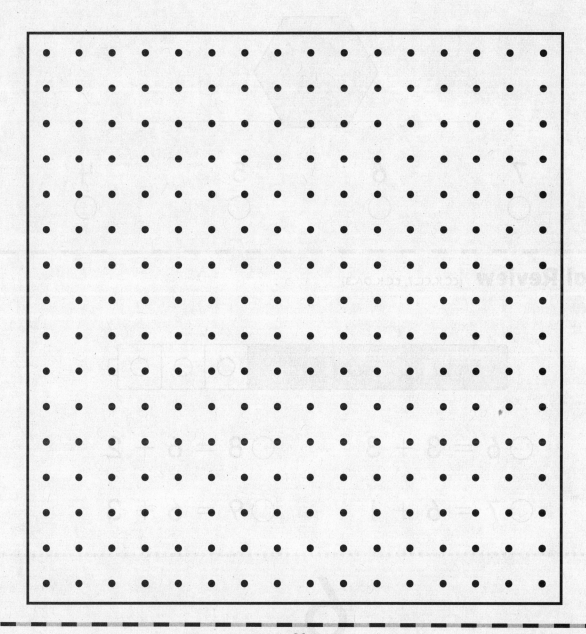

② _____

_ _ _ _ _

_____ **vertices**

③ _____

_ _ _ _ _

_____ **sides**

**DIRECTIONS** **1.** Draw and color a hexagon. **2.** Place a counter
on each corner, or vertex, of the hexagon that you drew. Write
how many corners, or vertices. **3.** Trace around the sides of the
hexagon that you drew. Write how many sides.

## Lesson Check (CC.K.G.4)

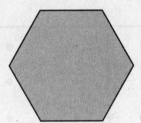

| 7 | 6 | 5 | 4 |
|---|---|---|---|
| ○ | ○ | ○ | ○ |

## Spiral Review (CC.K.CC.7, CC.K.OA.3)

○ 6 = 3 + 3          ○ 8 = 6 + 2

○ 7 = 6 + 1          ○ 9 = 6 + 3

# 6

| 4 | 7 | 5 | 6 |
|---|---|---|---|
| ○ | ○ | ○ | ○ |

**DIRECTIONS** **1.** How many sides does the hexagon have? Mark under your answer. **(Lesson 9.10)** **2.** Which addition sentence shows a number pair that matches the cube train? Mark beside your answer. **(Lesson 5.11)** **3.** Which number is greater than 6? Mark under your answer. **(Lesson 4.7)**

Name _____

# Algebra • Compare Two-Dimensional Shapes

**COMMON CORE STANDARD** CC.K.G.4
Analyze, compare, create, and compose shapes.

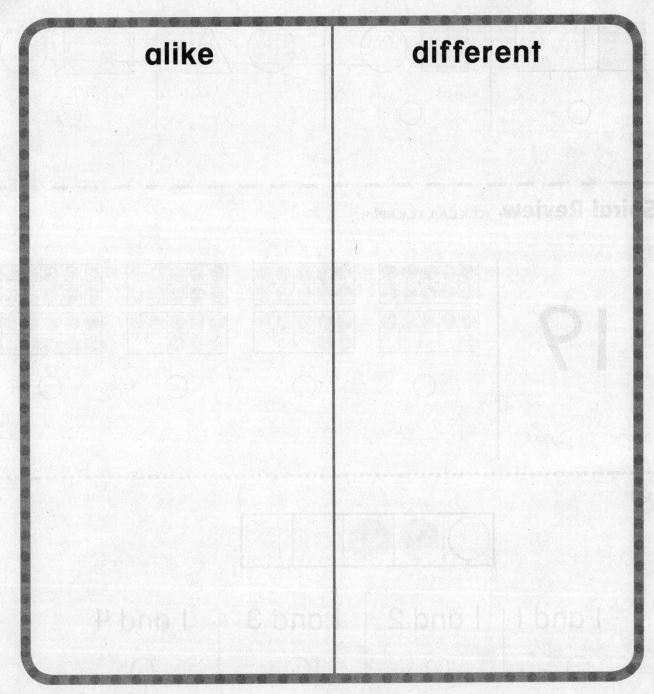

| alike | different |
| --- | --- |
|  |  |

**DIRECTIONS** 1. Place two-dimensional shapes on the page. Sort the shapes by the number of sides. Draw the shapes on the sorting mat. Use the words *alike* and *different* to tell how you sorted the shapes.

# Lesson Check (CC.K.G.4)

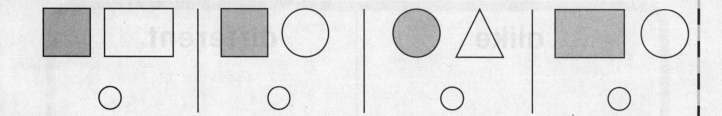

○          ○          ○          ○

# Spiral Review (CC.K.OA.1, CC.K.NBT.1)

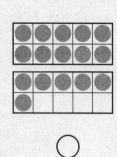  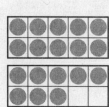 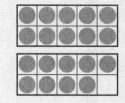

○          ○          ○          ○

| I and I | I and 2 | I and 3 | I and 4 |

○          ○          ○          ○

---

**DIRECTIONS** I. Which two shapes are alike in some way? Mark under your answer.
(Lesson 9.11)  **2.** Which set of counters shows the number 19? Mark under your
answer. (Lesson 7.9)  **3.** Which shows the gray counters being added to the five frame?
Mark under your answer. (Lesson 5.1)

**P192** one hundred ninety-two

# Problem Solving • Draw to Join Shapes

**COMMON CORE STANDARD** CC.K.G.6
Analyze, compare, create, and
compose shapes.

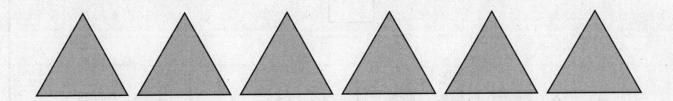

 **1**

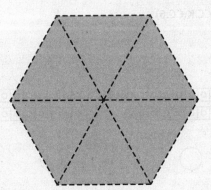

 **2**

**DIRECTIONS** 1. Place triangles on the page as shown. How can you join all of the triangles to make a hexagon? Trace around the triangles to draw the hexagon.
2. How can you join some of the triangles to make a larger triangle? Trace around the triangles to draw the larger triangle.

# Lesson Check (CC.K.G.6)

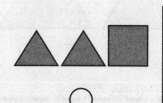   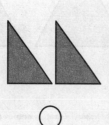   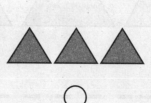   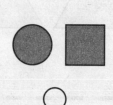

◯          ◯          ◯          ◯

# Spiral Review (CC.K.CC.5, CC.K.CC.6)

◯          ◯          ◯          ◯

3

| 5 | 6 | 7 | 8 |
|---|---|---|---|
| ◯ | ◯ | ◯ | ◯ |

**DIRECTIONS** 1. Which shapes could you join to make the rectangle above? Mark under your answer. **(Lesson 9.12)** 2. Which set of cubes models the number 20? Mark under your answer. **(Lesson 8.1)** 3. Mark under the number that is less than the number of spoons. **(Lesson 4.6)**

COMMON CORE STANDARDS CC.K.G.2,
CC.K.G.4, CC.K.G.6

# Chapter 9 Extra Practice

## Lessons 9.1 - 9.6 (pp. 357–379) · · · · · · · · · · · · · · · · · · · · · · · · · · ·

 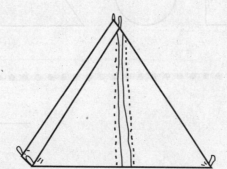 

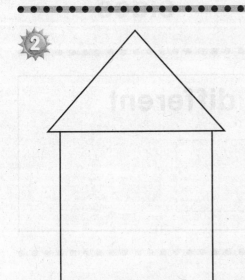  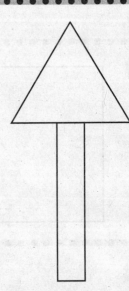

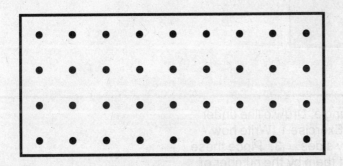

**DIRECTIONS** 1. Color the object that is shaped like a
circle. 2. Use red to color the squares in the picture. Use
green to color the triangles. 3. Draw and color a triangle.

**1**

● ● ● ● ● ● ● ● ● ● ● ● ● ● ● ● ● ● ● ● ● ● ● ● ● ● ● ● ● ● ● ● ● ● ● ● ● ●

**2**

_____          _____

- - - - - - - -               - - - - - - - -

_____ **vertices**          _____ **sides**

● ● ● ● ● ● ● ● ● ● ● ● ● ● ● ● ● ● ● ● ● ● ● ● ● ● ● ● ● ● ● ● ● ● ● ● ● ●

**3**

| alike | different |
|---|---|

● ● ● ● ● ● ● ● ● ● ● ● ● ● ● ● ● ● ● ● ● ● ● ● ● ● ● ● ● ● ● ● ● ● ● ● ● ●

**4**

**DIRECTIONS** 1. Mark an X on the rectangle. Draw a line under the hexagon. 2. Look at the hexagon in Exercise 1. Write how many corners, or vertices. Write how many sides. 3. Place these two-dimensional shapes on the page. Sort them by the number of vertices as shown. Trace the shapes. Color the shapes that have three vertices. 4. Place two squares on the page as shown. How can you join the squares to make a rectangle? Trace around the squares to draw the rectangle.

# School-Home
# Letter

## Dear Family,

My class started Chapter 10 this week. In this chapter, I will learn how identifying and describing shapes can help me sort them.

Love, _____

## Vocabulary

**sphere** a three-dimensional shape that is round
A ball is an example of a sphere.

**cylinder** a three-dimensional shape with a curved surface and two flat surfaces

## Home Activity

Take a walk around your neighborhood with your child. Ask your child to point out objects that are shaped like three-dimensional shapes, such as spheres, cubes, cylinders, and cones.

Recycle

## Literature

Look for these books at the library. The pictures will help your child understand how shapes are a part of everyday life.

**What in the World Is a Sphere?**
by Anders Hanson. SandCastle, 2007.

**Cubes, Cones, Cylinders, & Spheres**
by Tana Hoban. Greenwillow Books, 2000.

# Carta
## para la casa

## Querida familia:

Mi clase comenzó el Capítulo 10 esta semana. En este capítulo, aprenderé cómo identi car y describir  guras puede ayudarme a clasi carlas.

Con cariño, _____

## Vocabulario

**esfera** una figura tridimensional redonda

Una pelota es un ejemplo de esfera.

**cilindro** una figura tridimensional con una superficie curva y dos superficies planas

## Actividad para la casa

Salga a caminar por el barrio junto a su hijo. Pídale que señale objetos que tengan formas tridimensionales, tales como esferas, cubos, cilindros y conos.

## Literatura

Busque estos libros en la biblioteca. Los dibujos ayudarán a que su hijo comprenda cómo las figuras forman parte de la vida diaria.

**What in the World Is a Sphere?** por Anders Hanson. SandCastle, 2007.

**Cubes, Cones, Cylinders & Spheres** por Tana Hoban. Greenwillow Books, 2000.

# Three-Dimensional Shapes

COMMON CORE STANDARD CC.K.G.4
Analyze, compare, create, and compose shapes.

 **1**

**roll**

---

 **2**

**stack**

---

 **3**

**slide**

---

 **4**

**stack and slide**

**DIRECTIONS** 1. Which shape does not roll? Mark an X on that shape. 2. Which shapes do not stack? Mark an X on those shapes. 3. Which shape does not slide? Mark an X on that shape. 4. Which shape does not stack and slide? Mark an X on that shape.

## Lesson Check (CC.K.G.4)

## Spiral Review (CC.K.CC.2, CC.K.G.4)

○ 17, 20, 19, 18          ○ 17, 18, 20, 19

○ 20, 19, 17, 18          ○ 17, 18, 19, 20

**DIRECTIONS** **1.** Which shape does not roll? Mark under your answer. **(Lesson 10.1)** **2.** Which set of numbers is in order? Mark beside your answer. **(Lesson 8.3)** **3.** Which shape has a curve? Mark under your answer. **(Lesson 9.2)**

# Identify, Name, and Describe Spheres

**COMMON CORE STANDARD** CC.K.G.2
Identify and describe shapes (squares, circles, triangles, rectangles, hexagons, cubes, cones, cylinders, and spheres).

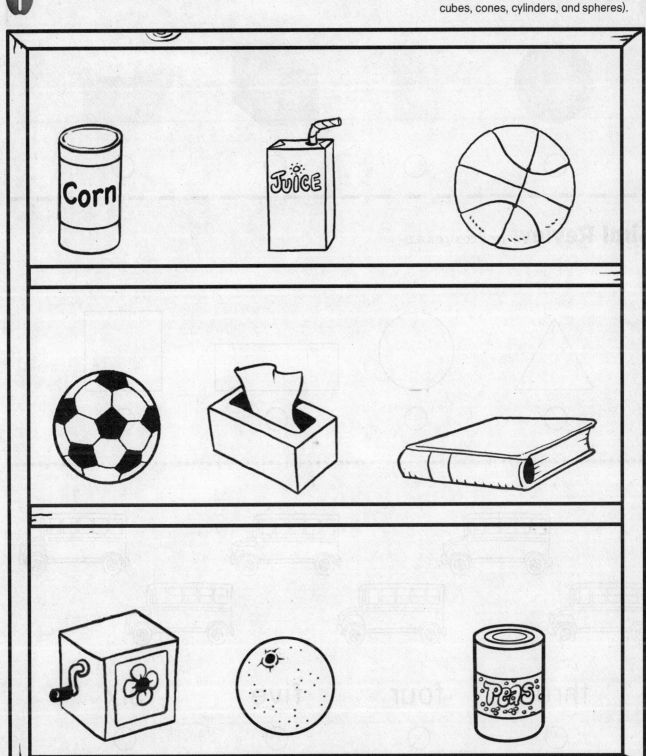

**DIRECTIONS** 1. Identify the objects that are shaped like a sphere. Mark an X on those objects.

○     ○     ○     ○

## Spiral Review <small>(CC.K.CC.3, CC.K.G.2)</small>

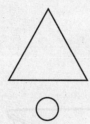 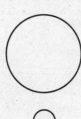  

○     ○     ○     ○

three     four     five     six

○     ○     ○     ○

---

**DIRECTIONS**   **1.** Which shape is a sphere? Mark under your answer. **(Lesson 10.2)**
**2.** Which shape is a square? Mark under your answer. **(Lesson 9.3)**
**3.** How many school buses are there? Mark under your answer. **(Lesson 3.2)**

Name _____

# Identify, Name, and Describe Cubes

**COMMON CORE STANDARD CC.K.G.2**
Identify and describe shapes (squares,
circles, triangles, rectangles, hexagons,
cubes, cones, cylinders, and spheres).

**DIRECTIONS**   **I.** Identify the objects that are shaped
like a cube. Mark an X on those objects.

## Lesson Check (CC.K.G.2)

○       ○       ○       ○

## Spiral Review (CC.K.CC.1, CC.K.G.4)

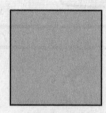

| 1 | 2 | 3 | 4 |
|---|---|---|---|
| ○ | ○ | ○ | ○ |

| 71 | 72 | 73 | 74 | 75 | 76 | 77 | 78 | 79 | 80 |
|----|----|----|----|----|----|----|----|----|-----|
| 81 | 82 | 83 | 84 | 85 | 86 | 87 | 88 | 89 | 90 |
| 91 | 92 | 93 | 94 | 95 | 96 | 97 | 98 | 99 | 100 |

| 89 | 91 | 98 | 100 |
|----|----|----|-----|
| ○ | ○ | ○ | ○ |

**DIRECTIONS  1.** Which shape is a cube? Mark under your answer. **(Lesson 10.3)**
**2.** How many sides does the square have? Mark under your answer. **(Lesson 9.4)**
**3.** Begin with 81 and count forward to 90. What is the next number? Mark under
your answer. **(Lesson 8.6)**

# Identify, Name, and Describe Cylinders

**COMMON CORE STANDARD** CC.K.G.2
Identify and describe shapes (squares, circles, triangles, rectangles, hexagons, cubes, cones, cylinders, and spheres).

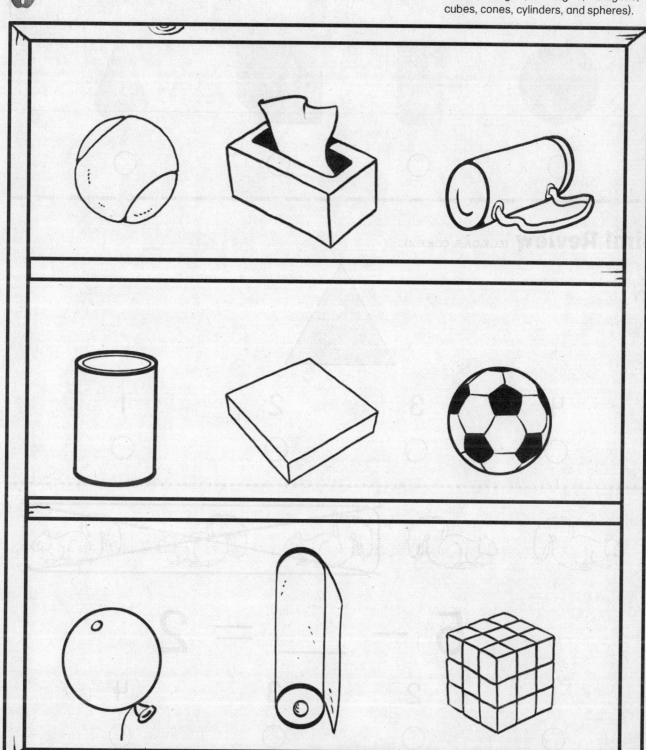

**DIRECTIONS** 1. Identify the objects that are shaped like a cylinder. Mark an X on those objects.

## Lesson Check (CC.K.G.2)

 1

 ○    ○    ○    ○

## Spiral Review (CC.K.OA.5, CC.K.G.4)

 2

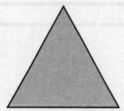

4          3          2          1

○          ○          ○          ○

3

$$5 - \underline{\phantom{0}} = 2$$

1          2          3          4

○          ○          ○          ○

---

**DIRECTIONS** **1.** Which shape is a cylinder? Mark under your answer. **(Lesson 10.4)**
**2.** How many vertices does the triangle have? Mark under your answer. **(Lesson 9.6)**
**3.** Mark under the number to show how many are being taken from the set. **(Lesson 6.5)**

Name _____

# Identify, Name, and Describe Cones

**COMMON CORE STANDARD** CC.K.G.2
Identify and describe shapes (squares, circles, triangles, rectangles, hexagons, cubes, cones, cylinders, and spheres).

**DIRECTIONS** 1. Identify the objects that are shaped like a cone. Mark an X on those objects.

**Chapter 10**

## Lesson Check (CC.K.G.2)

○          ○          ○          ○

## Spiral Review (CC.K.NBT.1, CC.K.G.2)

# 13

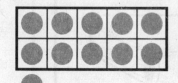   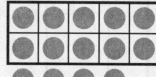

○          ○          ○          ○

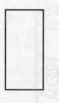   

○          ○          ○          ○

---

**DIRECTIONS** 1. Which shape is a cone? Mark under your answer. (Lesson 10.5)
2. Which set of counters shows the number 13? Mark under your answer. (Lesson 7.3)
3. Which shape is a circle? Mark under your answer. (Lesson 9.1)

Name _____

# Problem Solving • Two- and Three-Dimensional Shapes

COMMON CORE STANDARD CC.K.G.3
Identify and describe shapes (squares, circles, triangles, rectangles, hexagons, cubes, cones, cylinders, and spheres).

 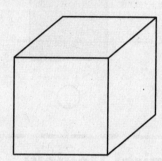

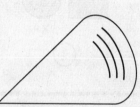

 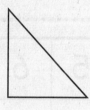

  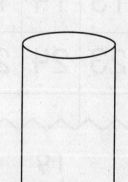 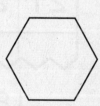

**DIRECTIONS   1.** Identify the two-dimensional or flat shapes. Use red to color the flat shapes. Identify the three-dimensional or solid shapes. Use blue to color the solid shapes.

**Chapter 10**

## Lesson Check (CC.K.G.3)

 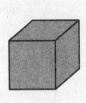  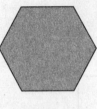

◯      ◯      ◯      ◯

## Spiral Review (CC.K.CC.1, CC.K.G.6)

 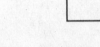  

◯      ◯      ◯      ◯

| 1 | 2 | 3 | 4 | 5 | 6 | 7 | 8 | 9 | 10 |
| 11 | 12 | 13 | 14 | 15 | 16 | 17 | 18 | 19 | 20 |
| 21 | 22 | 23 | 24 | 25 | 26 | 27 | 28 | 29 | 30 |

18      19      20      21

◯      ◯      ◯      ◯

**DIRECTIONS** 1. Which is a three-dimensional or solid shape? Mark
under your answer. **(Lesson 10.6)** 2. Which shapes could you join to make
the square above? Mark under your answer. **(Lesson 9.12)** 3. Begin with
1 and count forward to 19. What is the next number? Mark under your
answer. **(Lesson 8.5)**

# Above and Below

COMMON CORE STANDARD CC.K.G.1
Identify and describe shapes (squares, circles, triangles, rectangles, hexagons, cubes, cones, cylinders, and spheres).

**DIRECTIONS** **I.** Mark an X on the object that is shaped like a sphere below the table. Circle the object that is shaped like a cube above the table.

## Lesson Check (CC.K.G.1)

## Spiral Review (CC.K.CC.5, CC.K.G.4)

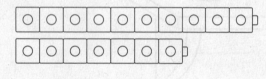    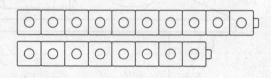

◯                ◯

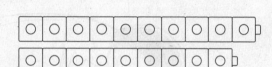

◯                ◯

5            6            7            8

◯            ◯            ◯            ◯

**DIRECTIONS** 1. Which picture shows that the object shaped like a sphere is above the box? Mark under your answer. **(Lesson 10.7)** 2. Which set of cubes models the number 20? Mark under your answer. **(Lesson 8.1)** 3. How many vertices does the hexagon have? Mark under your answer. **(Lesson 9.10)**

# Beside and Next To

COMMON CORE STANDARD CC.K.G.1
Identify and describe shapes (squares, circles, triangles, rectangles, hexagons, cubes, cones, cylinders, and spheres).

**DIRECTIONS   I.** Mark an X on the object shaped like a cylinder that is next to the object shaped like a sphere. Circle the object shaped like a cone that is beside the object shaped like a cube. Use the words *next to* and *beside* to name the position of other shapes.

## Lesson Check (CC.K.G.1)

○　　　　○　　　　○　　　　○

## Spiral Review (CC.K.CC.3, CC.K.G.2)

 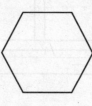  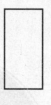

○　　　　○　　　　○　　　　○

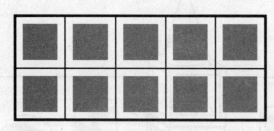 

16　　　　17　　　　18　　　　19

○　　　　○　　　　○　　　　○

**DIRECTIONS  1.** Which picture shows an object shaped like a sphere is beside an object shaped like a cylinder? Mark under your answer. **(Lesson 10.8)**
**2.** Which shape is a hexagon? Mark under your answer. **(Lesson 9.9)  3.** How many tiles are there? Mark under your answer. **(Lesson 7.10)**

# In Front Of and Behind

**COMMON CORE STANDARD** CC.K.G.1

Identify and describe shapes (squares, circles, triangles, rectangles, hexagons, cubes, cones, cylinders, and spheres).

**1**

**DIRECTIONS** **1.** Mark an X on the object shaped like a cylinder that is behind the object shaped like a cone. Draw a circle around the object shaped like a cylinder that is in front of the object shaped like a cube. Use the words *in front of* and *behind* to name the position of other shapes.

# Lesson Check (CC.K.G.1)

 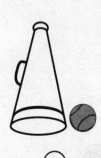  

◯ ◯ ◯ ◯

# Spiral Review (CC.K.OA.1, CC.K.G.2)

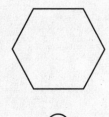  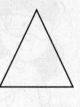 

◯ ◯ ◯ ◯

3 and 0     3 and 1     3 and 2     3 and 3

◯     ◯     ◯     ◯

**DIRECTIONS** **1.** Which picture shows an object shaped like a sphere in front of an object shaped like a cone? Mark under your answer. **(Lesson 10.9)**
**2.** Which shape is a triangle? Mark under your answer. **(Lesson 9.5)**
**3.** Which shows the gray counters being added to the five frame? Mark under your answer. **(Lesson 5.1)**

COMMON CORE STANDARDS CC.K.G.1, CC.K.G.2, CC.K.G.3, CC.K.G.4

# Chapter 10 Extra Practice

## Lessons 10.1 – 10.5 (pp. 413–432) · · · · · · · · · · · · · · · ·

· · · · · · · · · · · · · · · · · · · · · · · · · · · · · · · · · · · · ·

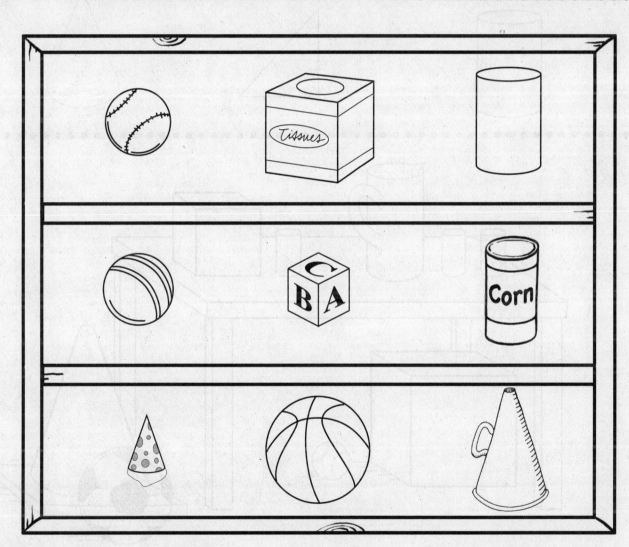

**DIRECTIONS** **I.** Which shapes do not stack? Mark an X on those shapes.
**2.** Identify the objects that are shaped like a sphere. Color those objects. Identify the objects that are shaped like a cube. Circle those objects. Identify the objects that are shaped like a cone. Mark an X on those objects. Identify the objects that are shaped like a cylinder. Draw a line under those objects.

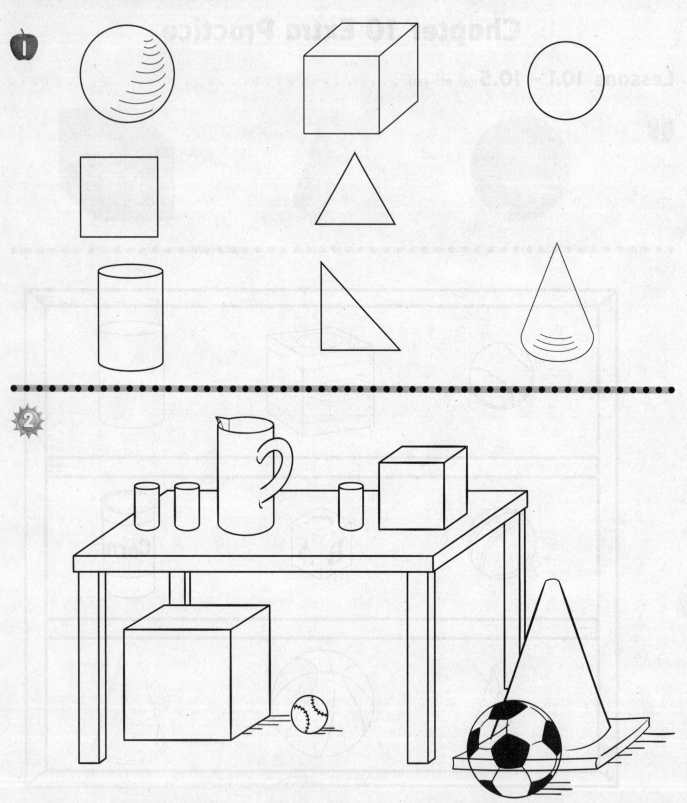

**DIRECTIONS** **1.** Identify the two-dimensional or flat shapes. Use red to color the flat shapes. Identify the three-dimensional or solid shapes. Use blue to color the solid shapes. **2.** Mark an X on the object shaped like a cube that is below the table. Draw a circle around the object shaped like a cylinder that is beside the object shaped like a cube. Color the object shaped like a sphere that is in front of the object shaped like a cone.

# School-Home Letter

## Dear Family,

My class started Chapter 11 this week. In this chapter, I will learn how comparing objects can help me measure them.

Love, _____

## Vocabulary

**longer** having a greater length

**heavier** having a greater weight

## Home Activity

Find two different-sized books. Ask your child to show you how to compare their lengths, heights, and weights.

## Literature

Look for these books at the library. Each book will give you ideas about how to enrich and encourage your child's measurement skills.

**How Long or How Wide?: A Measuring Guide** by Brian P. Cleary. Millbrook Press, 2007.

**Measurement (Beginning Skills)** by Amy Decastro. Teacher Created Resources, 2004.

# Carta
## para la casa

## Querida familia:

Mi clase comenzó el Capítulo 11 esta semana. En este capítulo, aprenderé cómo comparar objetos puede ayudarme a medirlos.

Con cariño, _____

## Vocabulario

**más largo que** que tiene mayor longitud

**más pesado** que tiene más peso

## Actividad para la casa

Busque 2 libros de diferentes tamaños. Pídale a su hijo que le muestre cómo comparar la longitud, la altura y el peso.

## Literatura

Busque estos libros en la biblioteca. Cada libro le dará ideas para enriquecer y alentar las destrezas de medición de su hijo.

**How Long or How Wide?: A Measuring Guide** por Brian P. Cleary. Millbrook Press, 2007.

**Measurement (Beginning Skills)** por Amy Decastro. Teacher Created Resources, 2004.

Name _____

# Compare Lengths

**COMMON CORE STANDARD** CC.K.MD.2
Describe and compare
measurable attributes.

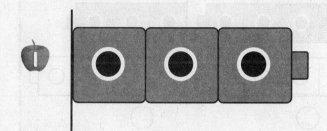

**DIRECTIONS** **1.** Make a cube train that is longer than the cube train shown.
Draw and color the cube train. **2.** Make a cube train that is shorter than the
cube train shown. Draw and color the cube train. **3.** Make a cube train that is
about the same length as the cube train shown. Draw and color the cube train.

**Chapter 11**

## Lesson Check (CC.K.MD.2)

**1**

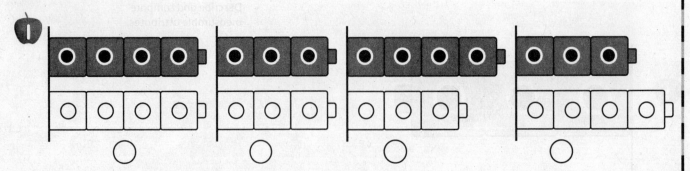

## Spiral Review (CC.K.G.2, CC.K.G.4)

**2**

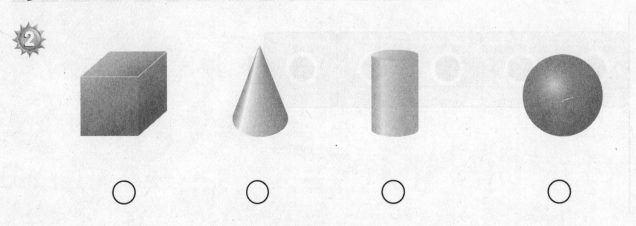

**3**

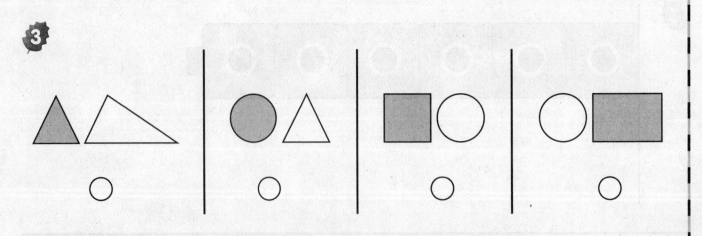

**DIRECTIONS** **I.** Which picture shows that the gray cube train is longer than the white cube train? Mark under your answer. (Lesson 11.1) **2.** Which shape is a sphere? Mark under your answer. (Lesson 10.2) **3.** Which two shapes each have three sides? Mark under your answer. (Lesson 9.11)

Name _____

# Compare Heights

**COMMON CORE STANDARD  CC.K.MD.2**
Describe and compare
measurable attributes.

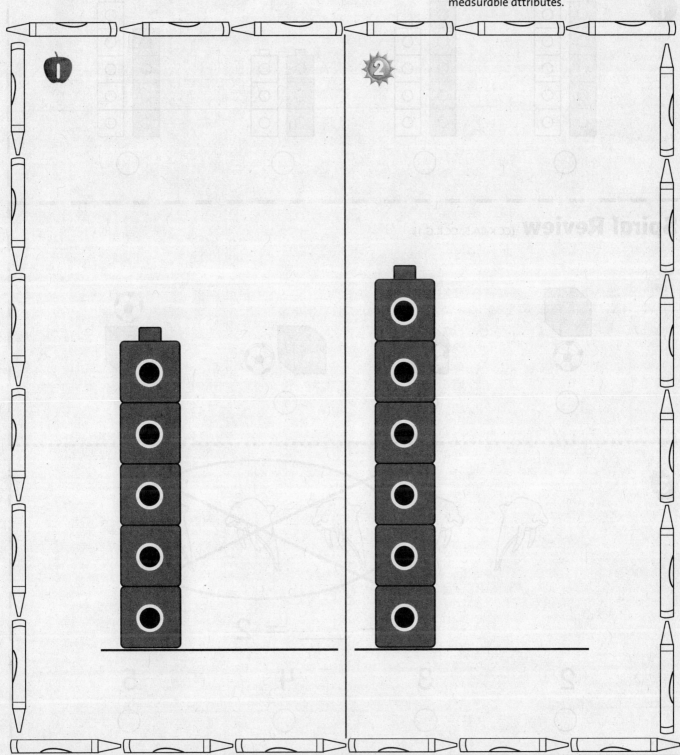

**1**

**2**

**DIRECTIONS**   **1.** Make a cube tower that is taller than the cube tower shown. Draw and color the cube tower.   **2.** Make a cube tower that is shorter than the cube tower shown. Draw and color the cube tower.

© Houghton Mifflin Harcourt Publishing Company

## Lesson Check (CC.K.MD.2)

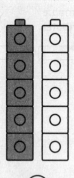

○        ○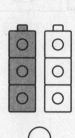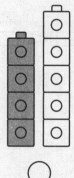

○        ○        ○        ○

## Spiral Review (CC.K.0A.5, CC.K.G.1)

○        ○        ○        ○

$$5 - \underline{\phantom{X}} = 2$$

2        3        4        5

○        ○        ○        ○

**DIRECTIONS** **1.** Which picture shows that the gray cube tower is shorter than the white cube tower? Mark under your answer. **(Lesson 11.2)** **2.** Which picture shows that the object shaped like a sphere is below the box? Mark under your answer. **(Lesson 10.7)** **3.** Mark under the number to show how many are being taken from the set. **(Lesson 6.5)**

Name _____

# Problem Solving • Direct Comparison

COMMON CORE STANDARD CC.K.MD.2
Describe and compare
measurable attributes.

 **1**

- - - - - - - - - - - - - - - - - - - - - - - - - - - - - - - - - - - -

**2**

**DIRECTIONS 1.** Find two small classroom objects. Place one end of each object on the line. Compare the lengths. Draw the objects. Say *longer than, shorter than,* or *about the same length* to describe the lengths. Circle the longer object. **2.** Find two small classroom objects. Place one end of each object on the line. Compare the heights. Draw the objects. Say *taller than, shorter than,* or *about the same height* to describe the heights. Circle the shorter object.

# Lesson Check (CC.K.MD.2)

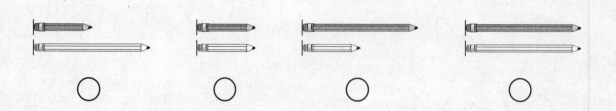

○     ○     ○     ○

# Spiral Review (CC.K.OA.2, CC.K.G.4)

4    3    2    I

○    ○    ○    ○

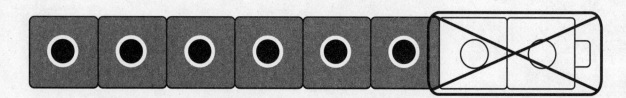

$2 + 6 = 8$ | $6 + 2 = 8$ | $8 - 6 = 2$ | $8 - 2 = 6$

○     ○     ○     ○

**DIRECTIONS** **1.** Which picture shows that the gray pencil is longer than the white pencil? Mark under your answer. **(Lesson 11.3)** **2.** How many vertices does the rectangle have? Mark under your answer. **(Lesson 9.8)** **3.** Mark under the number sentence that matches the picture. **(Lesson 6.7)**

Name _____

# Compare Weights

COMMON CORE STANDARD CC.K.MD.2
Describe and compare
measurable attributes.

 **left**           **right**

**1**  |

**2**  |

**3**  |

**4**  |

**DIRECTIONS** Find the first object in the row, and hold it in your left hand. Find the rest of the objects in the row, and hold each object in your right hand.   **1–2.** Circle the object that is lighter than the object in your left hand.   **3–4.** Circle the object that is heavier than the object in your left hand.

# Lesson Check (CC.K.MD.2)

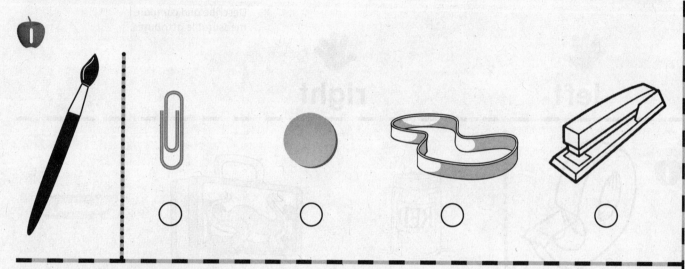

○      ○      ○      ○

# Spiral Review (CC.K.CC.6, CC.K.G.3)

② 

○      ○      ○      ○

③

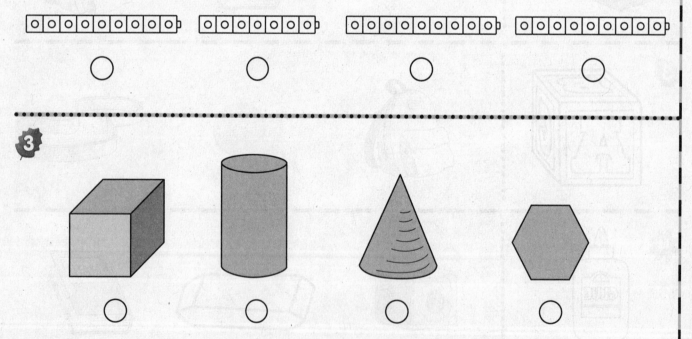

○      ○      ○      ○

**DIRECTIONS 1.** Which object is heavier than the paintbrush? Mark under your answer. **(Lesson 11.4)** **2.** Compare the cube trains. Mark under the cube train that has a number of cubes that is less. **(Lesson 4.5)** **3.** Which is a two-dimensional or flat shape? Mark under your answer. **(Lesson 10.6)**

Name _____

# Length, Height, and Weight

COMMON CORE STANDARD CC.K.MD.1
Describe and compare measurable attributes.

**DIRECTIONS** 1–4. Use red to trace the line that shows how to measure the length. Use blue to trace the line that shows how to measure the height. Talk about another way to measure the object.

**Chapter 11**

two hundred twenty-nine **P229**

# Lesson Check (CC.K.MD.1)

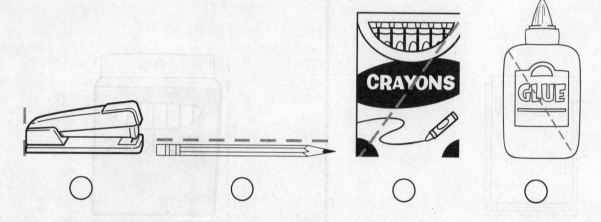

○          ○          ○          ○

# Spiral Review (CC.K.NBT.1, CC.K.G.2)

## 12

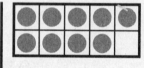 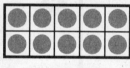 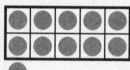 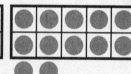

   ○          ○          ○          ○

 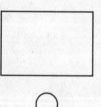 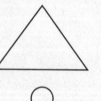 

○          ○          ○          ○

**DIRECTIONS** 1. Which picture shows how to measure the length of the object? Mark under your answer. (Lesson 11.5)  2. Which set of counters shows the number 12? Mark under your answer. (Lesson 7.1)  3. Which shape is a rectangle? Mark under your answer. (Lesson 9.7)

# Chapter 11 Extra Practice

## Lessons 11.1 - 11.3 (pp. 465–475)

**DIRECTIONS** 1. Make a cube train that is longer than the cube train shown. Draw and color the cube train. 2. Make a cube tower that is shorter than the cube tower shown. Draw and color the cube tower. 3. Find two small classroom objects. Place one end of each object on the line. Compare the lengths. Draw the objects. Say *longer than*, *shorter than*, or *about the same length* to describe the lengths. Circle the longer object.

**1**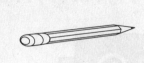

**2**

**3**

**DIRECTIONS** **1.** Find the first object in the row, and hold it in your left hand. Find the rest of the objects in the row, and hold each object in your right hand. Circle the object that is heavier than the object in your left hand. **2.** Find the first object in the row, and hold it in your left hand. Find the rest of the objects in the row, and hold each object in your right hand. Circle the object that is lighter than the object in your left hand. **3.** Use red to trace the line that shows how to measure the length. Use blue to trace the line that shows how to measure the height. Talk about another way to measure the object.

# School-Home Letter

## Dear Family,

My class started Chapter 12 this week. In this chapter, I will learn how sorting can help me display information.

Love, _____

## Vocabulary

**category**

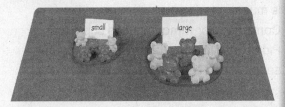

These bears are sorted and classified into two categories. One category is *small,* and one category is *large*.

## Home Activity

Have some fun in the kitchen as your child shows you all about sorting and classifying. Begin by collecting a handful of silverware. Have your child sort and classify it into groups by type of utensil.

## Literature

Look for these books at the library. Your child will continue learning while enjoying these great books.

**Sorting** by Henry Arthur Pluckrose. Children's Press, 1995.

**Grandma's Button Box** by Linda Williams Aber. Kane Press, 2002.

# Carta
## para la casa

# Querida familia:

Mi clase comenzó el Capítulo 12 esta semana. En este capítulo, aprenderé cómo clasi car puede ayudarme a mostrar información.

Con cariño, _____

## Vocabulario

**categoría**

Estos osos se clasifican en dos categorías. Una categoría es *osos pequeños* y la otra categoría es *osos grandes*.

## Actividad para la casa

Diviértanse en la cocina mientras su hijo le muestra todo sobre cómo clasificar. Comience por tomar algunos cubiertos. Pídale a su hijo que los clasifique en grupos según el tipo de utensilio.

## Literatura

Busque este libro en la biblioteca. Su hijo seguirá aprendiendo mientras disfruta de este excelente libro.

**Sorting**
por Henry Arthur Pluckrose.
Children's Press, 1995.

**Grandma's Button Box**
por Linda Williams Aber.
Kane Press, 2002

Name _____

# Algebra • Classify and Count by Color

**COMMON CORE STANDARD** CC.K.MD.3
Classify objects and count the number of objects in each category.

| yellow | red |
|--------|-----|

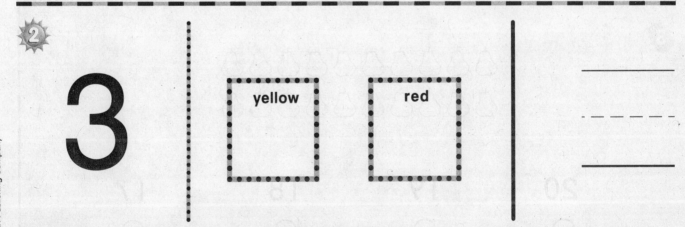

**3** | yellow | red |

**DIRECTIONS** **1.** Place a yellow square, red triangle, red rectangle, yellow square, and red triangle at the top of the page as shown. Sort and classify the shapes by the category of color. Draw and color the shapes in each category.   **2.** Look at the categories in Exercise 1. Count how many in each category. Circle the category that has 3 shapes. Write the number.

## Lesson Check (CC.K.MD.3)

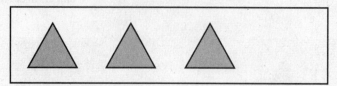

◯                    ◯                    ◯                    ◯

## Spiral Review (CC.K.CC.3, CC.K.G.4)

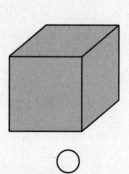                              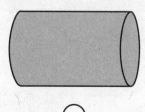

◯                    ◯                    ◯                    ◯

| 20 | 19 | 18 | 17 |
|----|----|----|----|
| ◯  | ◯  | ◯  | ◯  |

**DIRECTIONS** **I.** Look at the set of shapes. Which shape belongs in the same category? Mark under your answer. **(Lesson 12.1)** **2.** Which shape does not stack? Mark under your answer. **(Lesson 10.1)** **3.** Count and tell how many pieces of fruit. Mark under your answer. **(Lesson 8.2)**

Name _____

# Algebra • Classify and Count by Shape

COMMON CORE STANDARD CC.K.MD.3
Classify objects and count the number of objects in each category.

| triangle | circle |
|----------|--------|
|          |        |

**2**

| triangle | circle |
|----------|--------|
|          |        |

_____

- - - - - - -

**DIRECTIONS** **1.** Place a green triangle, blue circle, red triangle and blue circle at the top of the page as shown. Sort and classify the shapes by the category of shape. Draw and color the shapes in each category. **2.** Look at the categories in Exercise 1. Count how many in each category. Circle the categories that have two shapes. Write the number.

# Lesson Check (CC.K.MD.3)

   ○        ○        ○          ○

# Spiral Review (CC.K.OA.3, CC.K.MD.2)

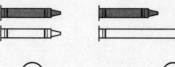

○          ○          ○          ○

○ 5 = 1 + 4     ○ 6 = 2 + 4

○ 5 = 2 + 3     ○ 6 = 5 + 1

**DIRECTIONS   1.** Look at the set of shapes. Which shape belongs in the same category? Mark under your answer. **(Lesson 12.2)   2.** Which picture shows that the gray crayon is shorter than the white crayon? Mark under your answer. **(Lesson 11.3)   3.** Which addition sentence shows a number pair that matches the cube train? Mark beside your answer. **(Lesson 5.8)**

Name _____

# Algebra • Classify and Count by Size

COMMON CORE STANDARD CC.K.MD.3
Classify objects and count the number of objects in each category.

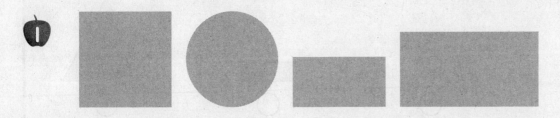

| small | big |
|-------|-----|
|       |     |

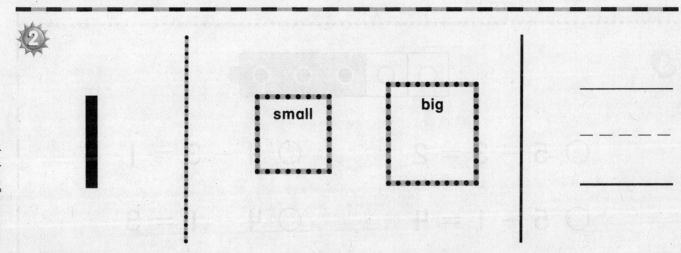

**DIRECTIONS** 1. Place a yellow square, blue circle, red rectangle, and blue rectangle at the top of the page as shown. Sort and classify the shapes by the category of size. Draw and color the shapes in each category. 2. Look at the categories in Exercise 1. Count how many in each category. Circle the category that has one per category. Write the number.

 1

         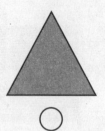

○      ○      ○      ○

**Spiral Review** (CC.K.OA.5, CC.K.G.2)

 2

| 1 | 2 | 3 | 4 |
|---|---|---|---|
| ○ | ○ | ○ | ○ |

 3

○ $5 - 3 = 2$          ○ $4 - 3 = 1$

○ $5 - 1 = 4$          ○ $4 - 1 = 3$

**DIRECTIONS** **1.** Look at the size of the shapes. Mark under the shape that does not belong. **(Lesson 12.3)** **2.** How many flat surfaces does the cylinder have? Mark under your answer. **(Lesson 10.4)** **3.** Sarah makes the cube train shown. She takes the cube train apart to show how many cubes are gray. Mark under the subtraction sentence that shows Sarah's cube train. **(Lesson 6.4)**

Name _____

# Make a Concrete Graph

**COMMON CORE STANDARD CC.K.MD.3**
Classify objects and count the number of
objects in each category.

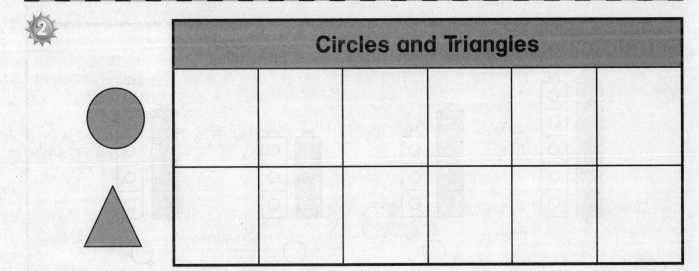

**DIRECTIONS** 1. Place a handful of green circles and triangles on the
workspace. Sort and classify the shapes by category. 2. Move the shapes
to the graph. Draw and color the shapes. 3. Write how many of each shape.

# Lesson Check (CC.K.MD.3)

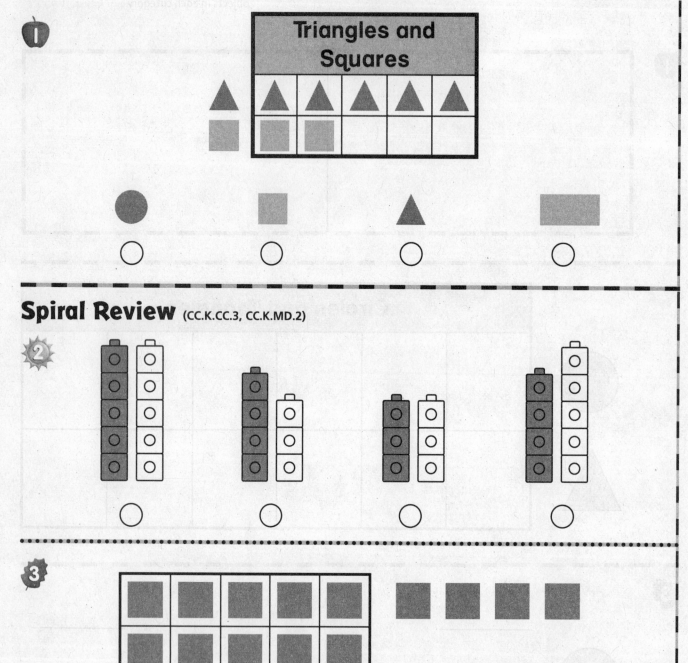

**1**

| Triangles and Squares | | | | | |
|---|---|---|---|---|---|
| ▲ | ▲ | ▲ | ▲ | ▲ | ▲ |
| ■ | ■ | ■ | | | |

● ○      ■ ○      ▲ ○      ▬ ○

# Spiral Review (CC.K.CC.3, CC.K.MD.2)

**2**      ○      ○      ○      ○

**3**

11 ○      12 ○      13 ○      14 ○

---

**DIRECTIONS  1.** Which row has five shapes? Mark under your answer. **(Lesson 12.4)**
**2.** Which picture shows that the gray cube tower is shorter than the white cube tower?
Mark under your answer. **(Lesson 11.2)  3.** How many tiles are there? Mark under your
answer **(Lesson 7.4)**

# Read a Graph

**COMMON CORE STANDARD** CC.K.MD.3
Classify objects and count the number of
objects in each category.

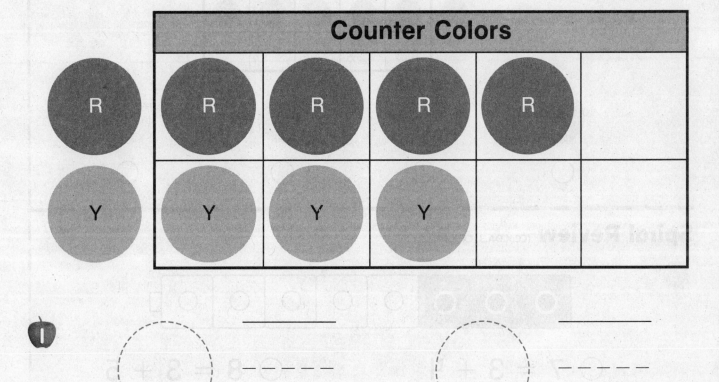

**DIRECTIONS** 1. Color the counters to show the categories.
R is for red, and Y is for yellow. How many counters are in each
category? Write the numbers. 2. Circle the category that has more
counters on the graph.

## Lesson Check (CC.K.MD.3)

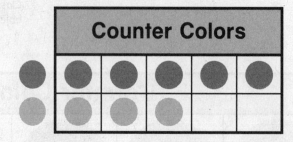

◯          ◯          ◯          ◯

## Spiral Review (CC.K.OA.3, CC.K.MD.2)

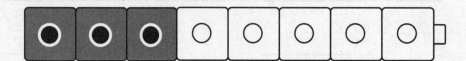

◯ 7 = 3 + 4          ◯ 8 = 3 + 5

◯ 7 = 6 + 1          ◯ 8 = 6 + 2

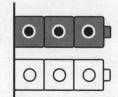     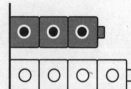     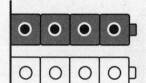     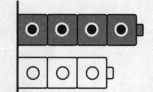

◯          ◯          ◯          ◯

**DIRECTIONS** **1.** Which category has more counters? Mark under your answer. **(Lesson 12.5)** **2.** Which addition sentence shows a numbers pair that matches the cube train? Mark beside your answer. **(Lesson 5.10)** **3.** In which picture is the gray cube train shorter than the white cube train? **(Lesson 11.1)**

# Problem Solving • Sort and Count

**COMMON CORE STANDARD** CC.K.MD.3
Classify objects and count the number of objects in each category.

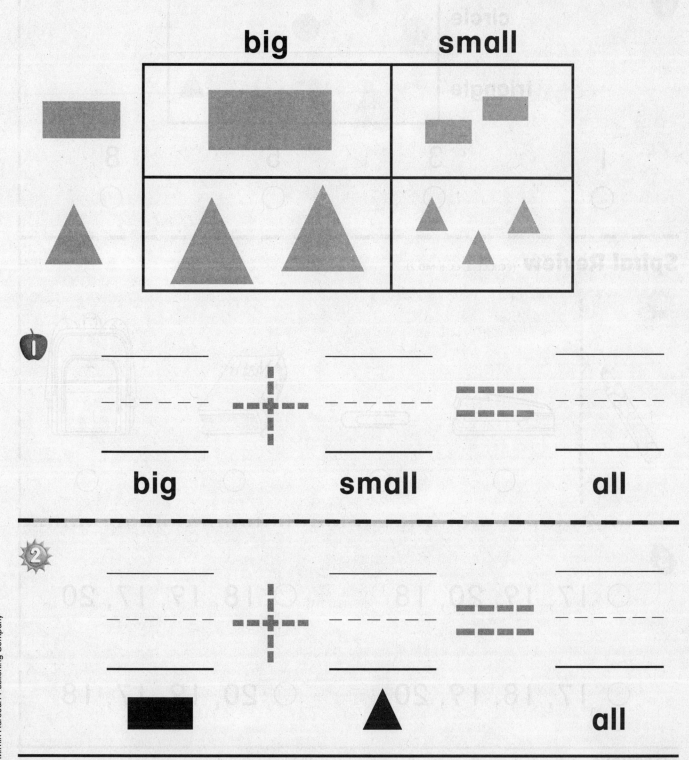

## big          small

## big     +     small     =     all

---

2      _____     +     _____     =     _____

all

---

**DIRECTIONS** Explain how the shapes are sorted.   **1.** How many big and small shapes are shown? Write and trace to complete the addition sentence.   **2.** How many rectangles and triangles are shown? Write and trace to complete the addition sentence.

# Lesson Check (CC.K.MD.3)

**1**

circle

triangle

| 1 | 3 | 5 | 8 |
|---|---|---|---|
| ○ | ○ | ○ | ○ |

# Spiral Review (CC.K.CC.2, CC.K.MD.2)

**2**

 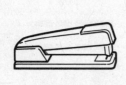   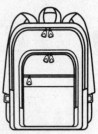

　　　　　　　○　　　　　○　　　　　○　　　　　○

**3**

○ 17, 19, 20, 18　　　　○ 18, 19, 17, 20

○ 17, 18, 19, 20　　　　○ 20, 19, 17, 18

**DIRECTIONS  1.** Look at the shapes on the sorting mat. Which number shows how many circles and triangles there are in all? Mark under your answer. **(Lesson 12.6)**
**2.** Which object is lighter than the marker? Mark under your answer. **(Lesson 11.4)**
**3.** Which set of numbers is in order? Mark beside your answer. **(Lesson 8.3)**

# Chapter 12 Extra Practice

## Lessons 12.1–12.3 (pp. 235–240) · · · · · · · · · · · · · · · · · ·

**1**

| rectangle | triangle |
|---|---|
|  |  |

**2**

2 │ rectangle │ triangle │ _____

**DIRECTIONS** 1. Place a red triangle, red rectangle, green triangle, red triangle, and blue rectangle at the top of the page as shown. Sort and classify the shapes by the category of shape. Draw and color the shapes in each category. Look at the categories in Exercise 1. Count how many in each category. **2.** Circle the category that has two shapes. Write the number.

## Counter Colors

| | R | R | | | |
|---|---|---|---|---|---|
| Y | Y | Y | Y | Y | Y |

**1**

**2**

triangle

square

all

---

**DIRECTIONS** 1. Color the counters to show the categories. R is for red, and Y is for yellow. How many counters are in each category? Write the numbers. 2. Look at the sorting mat. How are the shapes sorted? How many triangles are shown? How many squares are shown? Add the two sets. Write the numbers and trace the symbols to complete the addition sentence.

Name _____

# Add One

  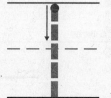 

**2**

**3**

**DIRECTIONS** **1.** Place cubes as shown above the numbers.
Trace the cubes. Trace to complete the addition sentence.
**2–3.** Use cubes to show the number. Draw the cubes.
Show and draw one more cube. Complete the addition sentence.

**Getting Ready for Grade 1**

4

$$5 + \underline{\quad\quad} = \underline{\quad\quad}$$

5

$$6 + \underline{\quad\quad} = \underline{\quad\quad}$$

6

$$7 + \underline{\quad\quad} = \underline{\quad\quad}$$

**DIRECTIONS 4–6.** Use cubes to show the number. Draw the cubes. Show and draw one more cube. Complete the addition sentence.

**HOME ACTIVITY •** Show your child a set of one to nine pennies. Have him or her use pennies to show how to add one to the set. Then have him or her tell how many in all.

_____  +  _____  =  _____

_____  +  _____  =  _____

_____  +  _____  =  _____

**ONS  4–6.** Count how many
e are. Write the number. Draw
shells. Complete the addition

**HOME ACTIVITY** • Draw objects in a column
beginning with a set of 1 to a set of 8. Have your
child draw two more objects beside each set,
and write how many in all.

two hundred fifty-two

# Add Two

**1**

$$1 + 2 = \underline{\quad}$$

---

**2**

$$\underline{\quad} + \underline{\quad} = \underline{\quad}$$

---

**3**

$$\underline{\quad} + \underline{\quad} = \underline{\quad}$$

---

**DIRECTIONS** **1.** Count how many shells in the first group. Trace the two shells. Trace to complete the addition sentence. **2–3.** Count how many shells. Write the number. Draw two more shells. Complete the addition sentence.

**Getting Ready for Grade 1**

two hu...

Name _____

# Add on a Ten Frame

| | | | | |
|---|---|---|---|---|
| red | red | red | red | red |
| yellow | yellow | yellow | yellow | yellow |

5 + 5 = 10

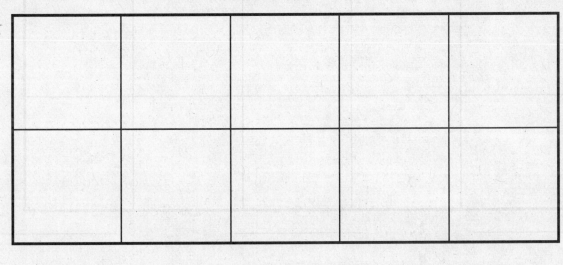

_____ + _____ = _____

**DIRECTIONS** 1. Place counters on the ten frame as shown. Trace the addition sentence. 2. Place some counters red side up on the ten frame. Add more counters yellow side up to fill the ten frame. Complete the addition sentence.

**Getting Ready for Grade 1**

two hundred fifty-three **P253**

**3**

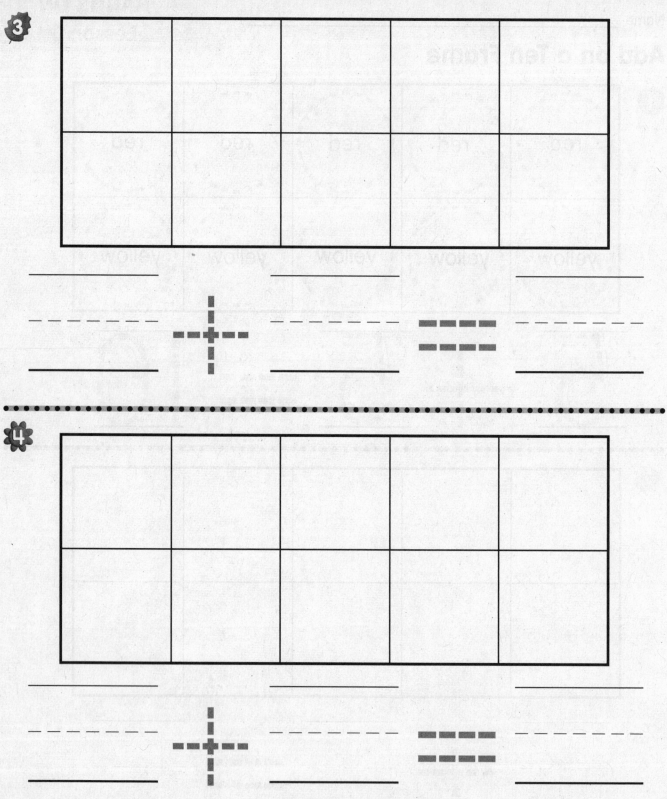

_____ _____  +  \_ \_ \_ \_ \_ \_ \_ \_  =  \_ \_ \_ \_ \_ \_ \_ \_

**4**

_____ _____ _____

\_ \_ \_ \_ \_ \_ \_ \_  +  \_ \_ \_ \_ \_ \_ \_ \_  =  \_ \_ \_ \_ \_ \_ \_ \_

**DIRECTIONS 3–4.** Place a different number of counters red side up on the ten frame. Add more counters yellow side up to fill the ten frame. Complete the addition sentence.

**HOME ACTIVITY** • Give your child some household objects, such as two different kinds of buttons. Have your child arrange the buttons to show different ways to make 10, such as 6 red buttons and 4 blue buttons. Write the addition sentence.

# Part-Part-Whole

**1** 

### Whole
### 2

### Part | Part

2 | 0

**2**

### Whole
### 3

### Part | Part

**DIRECTIONS** 1–2. How many cubes are there in all? Place that many cubes in the workspace. Show the parts that make the whole. Complete the chart to show all the parts that make the whole.

**Getting Ready for Grade 1**

two hundred fifty-five **P255**

## Whole
### 4

| Part | Part |
|------|------|
| ———— | ———— |
| – – – – | – – – – |
| ———— | ———— |
| – – – – | – – – – |
| ———— | ———— |
| – – – – | – – – – |
| ———— | ———— |
| – – – – | – – – – |
| ———— | ———— |
| – – – – | – – – – |
| ———— | ———— |

## Whole
### 5

| Part | Part |
|------|------|
| ———— | ———— |
| – – – – | – – – – |
| ———— | ———— |
| – – – – | – – – – |
| ———— | ———— |
| – – – – | – – – – |
| ———— | ———— |
| – – – – | – – – – |
| ———— | ———— |
| – – – – | – – – – |
| ———— | ———— |
| – – – – | – – – – |
| ———— | ———— |

**DIRECTIONS 3–4.** How many cubes are there in all? Complete the chart to show all the parts that make the whole.

**HOME ACTIVITY** • Have your child use buttons or macaroni pieces to show the different parts that make the whole set of 8 (e.g. 7 and 1, 6 and 2, 5 and 3, 4 and 4.)

Name _____

# Equal Sets

**1**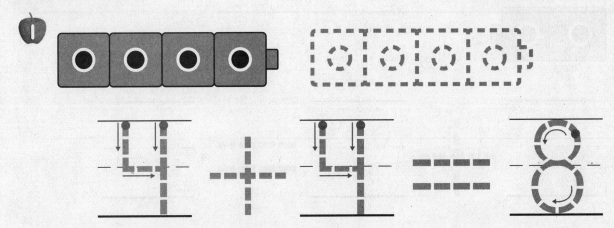

**2**

**3**

**DIRECTIONS** Count the cubes. Use cubes to make an equal set.
**1.** Trace the cubes. Trace the addition sentence. **2–3.** Draw the cubes. Write and trace to complete the addition sentence.

**Getting Ready for Grade 1**

_____ + _____ = _____
_____   _____   _____

- - - - - - - - - - - - - - - - - - - - - - - - - - - - - - -

- - - - - - - - - - - - - - - - - - - - - - - - - - - - - - -

**6**

**DIRECTIONS  4–6.** Count the cubes. Use cubes to make an equal set. Draw the cubes. Write and trace to complete the addition sentence.

**HOME ACTIVITY** • Have your child show equal sets by holding up an equal number of fingers on each hand. Then have your child say the addition sentence.

# ✓ Checkpoint

## Concepts and Skills

 **1**

$$4 + \underline{\hspace{2cm}} = \underline{\hspace{2cm}}$$

•••••••••••••••••••••••••••••••••••••••••••••

 **2**

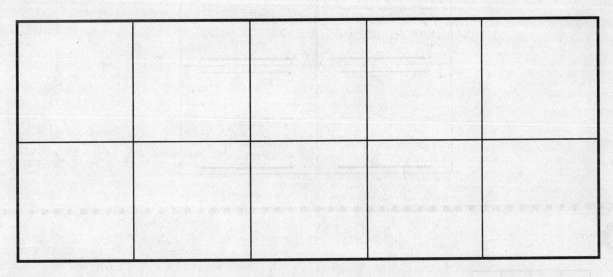

$$\underline{\hspace{2cm}} + \underline{\hspace{2cm}} = \underline{\hspace{2cm}}$$

---

**DIRECTIONS   1.** Use cubes to show the number. Draw the cubes. Show and draw one more cube. Complete the addition sentence. **(pp. P249–P250)   2.** Place some counters red side up on the ten frame. Add more counters yellow side up to fill the ten frame. Complete the addition sentence. **(pp. P253–P254)**

**3**

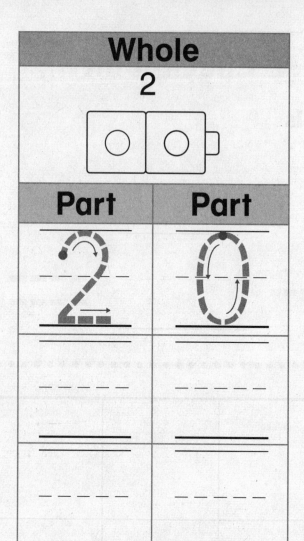

| Whole |
|:-:|
| 2 |

| Part | Part |
|:-:|:-:|
| 2 | 0 |
| | |
| | |

---

**DIRECTIONS 3.** How many cubes are there in all? Place that many cubes in the workspace. Show the different parts that make the whole. Complete the chart to show all the parts that make the whole. **(P55-P256) 4.** Count the cubes. Use cubes to make an equal set. Draw the cubes. Trace and write to complete the addition sentence. **(P257-P258)**

Name _____

# Related Addition Equations

$1 + 3 = 2 + 2$

___ + ___ = ___ + ___

___ + ___ = ___ + ___

**DIRECTIONS** Look at the cube trains. **1.** Trace to complete the equation. **2–3.** Trace and write to complete the equation.

**Getting Ready for Grade 1**

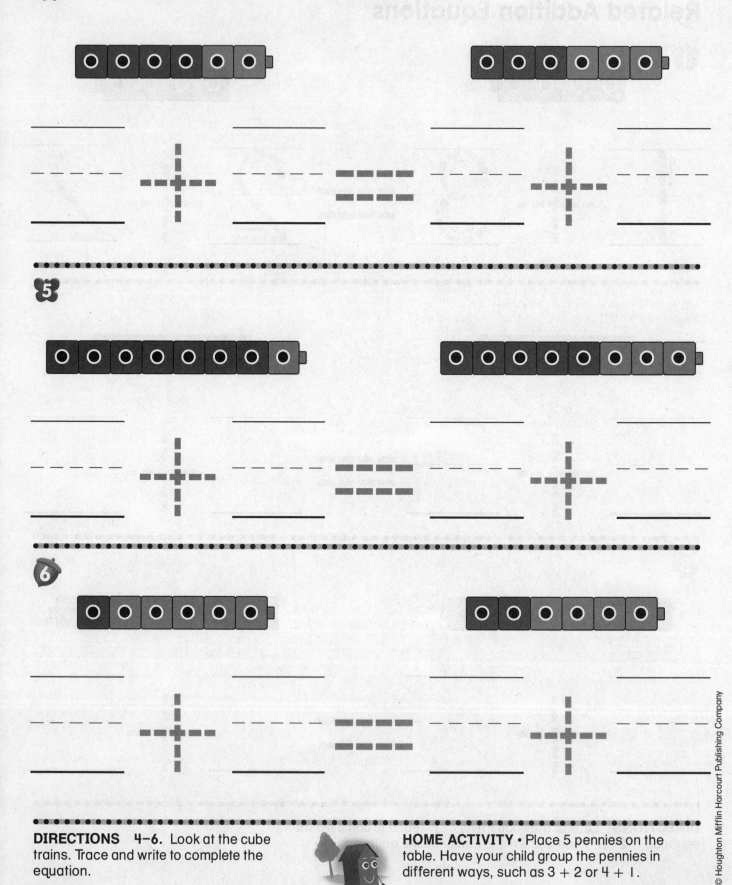

**4**

_____ _____    _____ _____

- - - -   **+**   _ _ _ _   **=**   - - - -   **+**   _ _ _ _

_____ _____    _____ _____

**5**

_____ _____    _____ _____

- - - -   **+**   _ _ _ _   **=**   - - - -   **+**   _ _ _ _

_____ _____    _____ _____

**6**

_____ _____    _____ _____

- - - -   **+**   _ _ _ _   **=**   - - - -   **+**   _ _ _ _

_____ _____    _____ _____

**DIRECTIONS  4–6.** Look at the cube trains. Trace and write to complete the equation.

**HOME ACTIVITY •** Place 5 pennies on the table. Have your child group the pennies in different ways, such as 3 + 2 or 4 + 1.

Name _____

# Subtract One

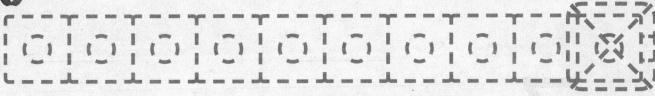

10 --- 1 == 9

9 --- _____ == _____

8 --- _____ == _____

**DIRECTIONS** **1.** Place cubes on the ones shown. Trace the cubes. Trace the circle and X on the cube being taken away. Trace to complete the subtraction sentence. **2–3.** Use cubes to show the number. Draw the cubes. Take away one cube. Circle the cube that you took away and mark an X on it. Complete the subtraction sentence.

**Getting Ready for Grade 1**                    two hundred sixty-three **P263**

4

7 ---- _ _ _ _ === _ _ _ _

---

5

6 ---- _ _ _ _ === _ _ _ _

---

6

5 ---- _ _ _ _ === _ _ _ _

---

**DIRECTIONS** **4–6.** Use cubes to show the number. Draw the cubes. Take away one cube. Circle the cube that you took away and mark an X on it. Complete the subtraction sentence.

**HOME ACTIVITY** • Ask your child to use toys to demonstrate and describe the number pattern in the subtraction sentences on this page.

Name _____

# Subtract Two

   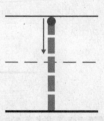

3 -- 2 == 1

_____ _____ == _____

_____ _____ == _____

**DIRECTIONS** **1.** Count how many boats there are in all. Trace the circle and the X that shows the boats that sail away. Trace to complete the subtraction sentence. **2–3.** Count how many boats there are in all. Write the number. Two boats sail away. Circle the boats that sail away. Mark an X on them. Complete the subtraction sentence.

**Getting Ready for Grade 1**

**4**

_____          _____          _____

\- \- \- \- \- \-     ▬▬▬▬     \- \- \- \- \- \-     ▬▬▬     \- \- \- \- \- \-
_____                    _____     ▬▬▬     _____

---

**5**

_____          _____          _____

\- \- \- \- \- \-     ▬▬▬▬     \- \- \- \- \- \-     ▬▬▬     \- \- \- \- \- \-
_____                    _____     ▬▬▬     _____

---

**6**

_____          _____          _____

\- \- \- \- \- \-     ▬▬▬▬     \- \- \- \- \- \-     ▬▬▬     \- \- \- \- \- \-
_____                    _____     ▬▬▬     _____

---

**DIRECTIONS   4–6.** Count how many boats there are in all. Write the number. Two boats sail away. Circle the boats that sail away.  Mark an X on them. Complete the subtraction sentence.

**HOME ACTIVITY** • Give your child five buttons. Have your child take away two buttons and tell how many are left.

# Subtract on a Ten Frame

**1**

| | | | | |
|---|---|---|---|---|
| red | red | red | red | red |
| red | red | red | red | red |

10 - 4 = 6

**2**

| | | | | |
|---|---|---|---|---|
| | | | | |
| | | | | |

_____    _____    _____

- - - - -    ====    - - - - -
                     ====

_____    _____    _____

**DIRECTIONS  I.** Place 10 counters as shown on the ten frame. Take away 4 counters. Trace the circle around the set of counters that you took away. Trace the X on that set. Trace the subtraction sentence. **2.** Place 10 counters on the ten frame. Draw the counters. Take away some counters. Circle the set of counters that you took away. Mark an X on that set. Complete the subtraction sentence.

**3**

_____          _____          _____

- - - - - - - - -     ▬ ▬ ▬ ▬     - - - - - - - - -     ▬ ▬ ▬ ▬     - - - - - - - - -
                                                        ▬ ▬ ▬ ▬

_____                     _____          _____

**4**

_____          _____          _____

- - - - - - - - -     ▬ ▬ ▬ ▬     - - - - - - - - -     ▬ ▬ ▬ ▬     - - - - - - - - -
                                                        ▬ ▬ ▬ ▬

_____                     _____          _____

**DIRECTIONS 3–4.** Place 10 counters on the ten frame. Draw the counters. Take away some counters. Circle the set of counters that you took away. Mark an X on that set. Complete the subtraction sentence.

**HOME ACTIVITY** • Give your child ten household objects, such as buttons. Have your child take some of the objects away. Then have him or her tell the subtraction sentence.

# Algebra: Missing Part

| Whole |
|:---:|
| **2** |
| 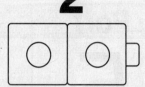 |

| Part | Part |
|:---:|:---:|
| **2** | 0 |
| **1** | _ _ _ _<br>____ |
| **0** | _ _ _ _<br>____ |

| Whole |
|:---:|
| **3** |

| Part | Part |
|:---:|:---:|
| **3** | _ _ _ _<br>____ |
| **2** | _ _ _ _<br>____ |
| **1** | _ _ _ _<br>____ |
| **0** | _ _ _ _<br>____ |

**DIRECTIONS** 1–2. How many cubes are there in all? Complete the chart to show the missing part that makes the whole.

**3**

| Whole |
|:---:|
| **4** |

| Part | Part |
|:---:|:---:|
| **4** | _____ |
| **3** | _____ |
| **2** | _____ |
| **1** | _____ |
| **0** | _____ |

**4**

| Whole |
|:---:|
| **5** |

| Part | Part |
|:---:|:---:|
| **5** | _____ |
| **4** | _____ |
| **3** | _____ |
| **2** | _____ |
| **1** | _____ |
| **0** | _____ |

**DIRECTIONS   3–4.** How many cubes are there in all? Complete the chart to show the missing part that makes the whole.

**HOME ACTIVITY** • Place 8 spoons on the table. Cover 3 of the spoons. Tell your child that you started with 8 spoons. Ask him or her to tell you how many spoons are covered.

© Houghton Mifflin Harcourt Publishing Company

# Related Subtraction Equations

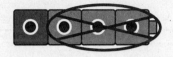

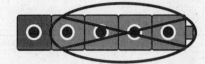

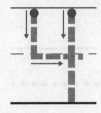 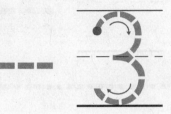 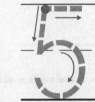 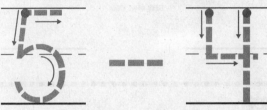

$$4 - 3 = 5 - 4$$

---

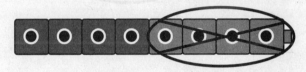

---

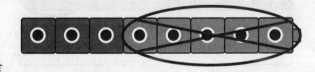

---

**DIRECTIONS** Look at the cube trains. **1.** Trace to complete the equation.
**2–3.** Trace and write to complete the equation.

**Getting Ready for Grade 1**

**4**

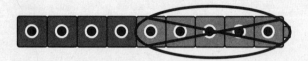          

_____  _____          _____  _____

- - - ▪▪▪ - - -   ▪▪▪▪ ▪▪▪▪   - - - ▪▪▪ - - -
                  ▪▪▪▪ ▪▪▪▪

_____  _____          _____  _____

---

**5**

- - - - - -  _____          - - - - - -  _____

- - - ▪▪▪ - - -   ▪▪▪▪ ▪▪▪▪   - - - ▪▪▪ - - -
                  ▪▪▪▪ ▪▪▪▪

_____  _____          _____  _____

---

**6**

_____  _____          - - - - - -  _____

- - - ▪▪▪ - - -   ▪▪▪▪ ▪▪▪▪   - - - ▪▪▪ - - -
                  ▪▪▪▪ ▪▪▪▪

_____  _____          _____  _____

---

**DIRECTIONS   4–6.** Look at the cube trains. Trace and write to complete the equation.

**HOME ACTIVITY** • Say a subtraction fact with a difference of 2. Have your child say another subtraction fact with a difference of 2.

# Related Addition and Subtraction Equations

$$3 + 3 = 8 - 2$$

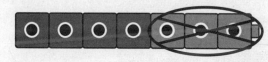 

**DIRECTIONS** Look at the cube trains. **1.** Trace to complete the equation.
**2–3.** Trace and write to complete the equation.

**Getting Ready for Grade 1**

two hundred seventy-three **P273**

**4**

_____  _____          _____  _____

– – –   **–**   – – –   **==**   – – –   **+**   – – –

_____  _____          _____  _____

- - - - - - - - - - - - - - - - - - - - - - - - - - - - - - - - - -

**5**

_____  _____          _____  _____

– – –   **–**   – – –   **==**   – – –   **+**   – – –

_____  _____          _____  _____

- - - - - - - - - - - - - - - - - - - - - - - - - - - - - - - - - -

_____  _____          _____  _____

– – –   **+**   – – –   **==**   – – –   **–**   – – –

_____  _____          _____  _____

- - - - - - - - - - - - - - - - - - - - - - - - - - - - - - - - - -

**DIRECTIONS** **4–6.** Look at the cube trains. Trace and write to complete the equation.

**HOME ACTIVITY** • Say an addition fact with a sum of 5. Then ask your child to say a subtraction fact with a difference of 5.

Name _____

# Subtract to Compare

**2** more 🔱

_____

_ _ _ _ _ _ _ _

_____ more 👓

**3**

_____

_ _ _ _ _ _ _ _

_____ more

**DIRECTIONS** **I.** Trace the lines to match the objects in the top row to the objects in the bottom row. Compare the sets. Trace the circle that shows the set with more objects. Trace the number. **2–3.** Draw lines to match the objects in the top row to the objects in the bottom row. Compare the sets. Circle the set that has more objects. Write how many more.

**Getting Ready for Grade 1**      two hundred seventy-five **P275**

**4**

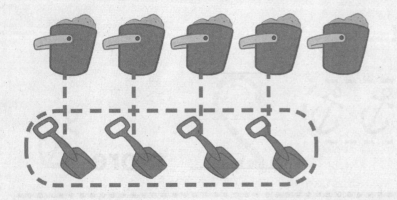

**fewer**

**5**

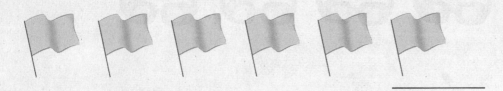

_____

- - - - - - - - -

_____ **fewer**

**6**

_____

- - - - - - - - -

_____ **fewer**

**DIRECTIONS** **4.** Trace the lines to match the objects in the top row to the objects in the bottom row. Compare the sets. Trace the circle that shows the set with fewer objects. Trace the number. **5–6.** Draw lines to match the objects in the top row to the objects in the bottom row. Compare the sets. Circle the set that has fewer objects. Write how many fewer.

**HOME ACTIVITY** • Show your child a row of seven pennies and a row of three nickels. Have your child compare the sets, identify which has fewer coins, and tell how many fewer. Repeat with other sets of coins up to ten.

Name _____

## Concepts and Skills

2  ___ ___

_ _ _ _ _ _ _    ▭▭▭    ___    ▭▭▭    _ _ _ _ _ _ _

___

| | | | | |
|---|---|---|---|---|
| | | | | |

___    ___

_ _ _ _ _ _    ▭▭    _ _ _ _ _ _    ▭▭▭    _ _ _ _ _ _
                                      ▭▭▭

___    ___

**DIRECTIONS** **1.** Use cubes to show the number. Draw the cubes. Take away one cube. Circle the cube that you took away and mark an X on it. Complete the subtraction sentence. **(P263–P264)** **2.** Place 10 counters on the ten frame. Draw the counters. Take away some counters. Circle and mark an X on the counters that you took away. Complete the subtraction sentence. **(P267–P268)**

© Houghton Mifflin Harcourt Publishing Company

**3**

_____  _____
- - - - -   ▬▬▬   - - - - -   ▬▬▬▬   - - - - -
_____              _____              ▬▬▬▬   _____

**4**

_____       _____       _____       _____
- - - ┼ - - -       ▬▬▬       - - - ┼ - - -
_____              _____              _____              _____

**5**

2          3          4          5
○          ○          ○          ○

**DIRECTIONS** **3.** Count and write how many boats in all. Two boats leave. Circle and mark an X on those boats. Complete the subtraction sentence. **(pp. P265–P266)** **4.** Look at the cube trains. Trace and write to complete the equation. **(pp. P261–P262)** **5.** Compare the sets. Mark under the number that shows how many more dogs are shown in the picture. **(pp. P275–P276)**

**P278** two hundred seventy-eight

Name _____

# Hands On: How Many Ones?

 **1**

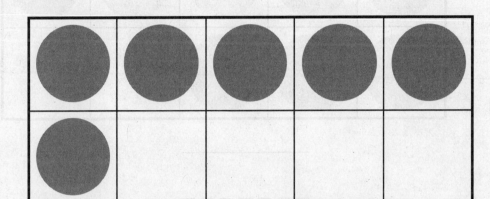

_ _ _ _ _ _ _ _

_____ **ones**

• • • • • • • • • • • • • • • • • • • • • • • • • • • • • • • • • • • • • •

**2**

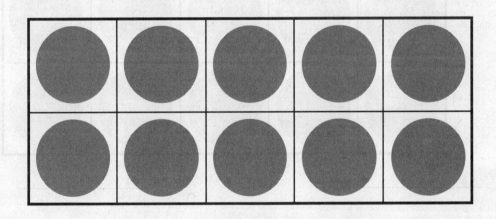

_____

_ _ _ _ _ _ _ _        or        _ _ _ _ _ _ _ _

_____ **ones   or** _____ **ten**

**DIRECTIONS**  Place counters on the ones shown.   **1.** How many ones are there? Write the number.   **2.** How many ones are there? Write the number.   How many tens is that? Write the number.

**3**

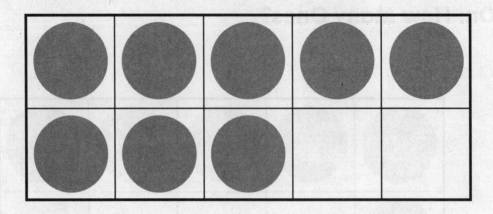

_____
_ _ _ _ _ _
_____ **ones**

**4**

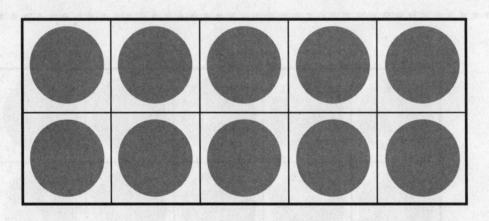

_____          _____
_ _ _ _ _        _ _ _ _ _
_____ **ones   or   _____ ten**

© Houghton Mifflin Harcourt Publishing Company

**DIRECTIONS** Place counters on the ones shown. **3.** How many ones are there? Write the number. **4.** How many ones are there? How many tens is that? Write the number.

**HOME ACTIVITY** • Place 10 small items on a table. Ask your child to count and write how many ones that is. Then ask him or her to write how many tens that is.

Name _____

# Read and Write Numbers 20 to 30

 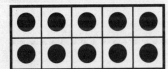 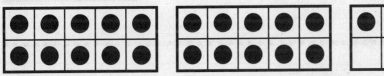 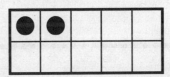 

   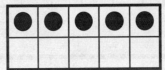

  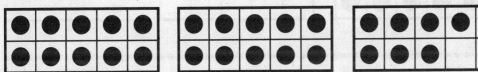 

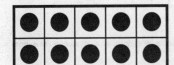 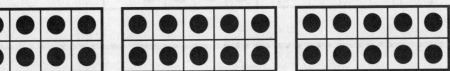 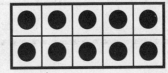

 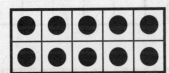 

**DIRECTIONS** How many counters are there? I. Trace the number.
2–5. Write the number.

**Getting Ready for Grade I**

**6**

**7**

**8**

**9**

**10**

**DIRECTIONS** 6–10. How many counters are there? Write the number.

**HOME ACTIVITY** • Give your child 20 to 30 paper clips. Have your child count the paper clips and write how many.

Name _____

# Read and Write Numbers 30 to 40

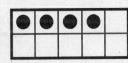
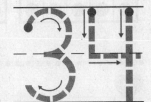

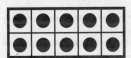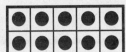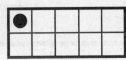

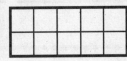

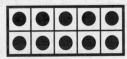

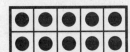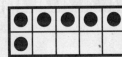

**DIRECTIONS** How many counters are there? **I.** Trace the number. **2–5.** Write the number.

**Getting Ready for Grade I**

two hundred eighty-three **P283**

**6**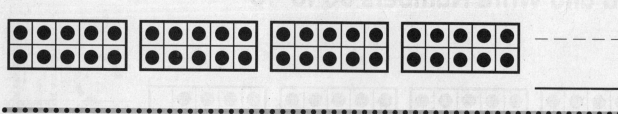

_____

_____

**7**

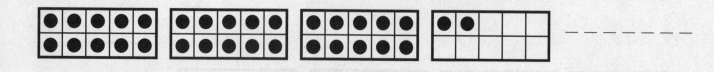

_____

_____

**8**

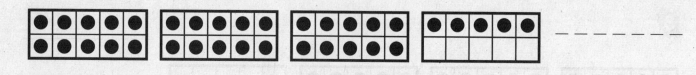

_____

_____

**9**

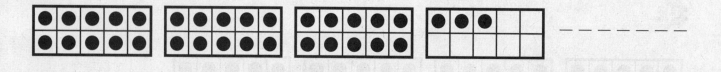

_____

_____

**10**

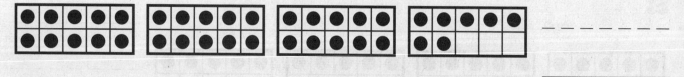

_____

_____

**DIRECTIONS   6–10.** How many counters are there? Write the number.

**HOME ACTIVITY** • Have your child count out cereal pieces for different numbers from 30 to 40.

Getting Ready for Grade 1

Name _____

# Read and Write Numbers 40 to 50

   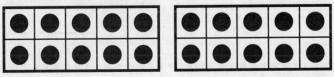 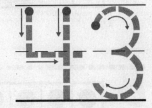

 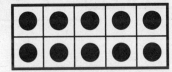  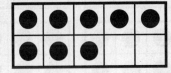

_____

_ _ _ _ _ _ _ _ _ _

_____

 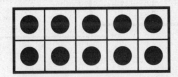 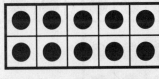 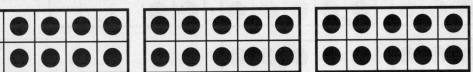

_____

_ _ _ _ _ _ _ _ _ _

_____

 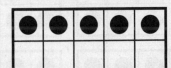

_____

_ _ _ _ _ _ _ _ _ _

_____

**DIRECTIONS**  How many counters are there? **1.** Trace the number.
**2–4.** Write the number.

**Getting Ready for Grade 1**                      two hundred eighty-five  **P285**

**5**

**6**

**7**

**8**

**DIRECTIONS** **5–8.** How many counters are there? Write the number.

**HOME ACTIVITY** • Help your child count four sets of ten cereal pieces each. Then have him or her tell how many cereal pieces there are.

**P286** two hundred eighty-six

#  Checkpoint

**1**

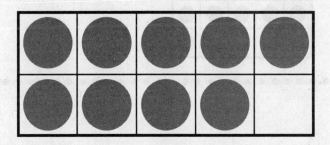

 ones

---

**2**

---

**3**

 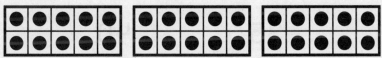

---

**DIRECTIONS** 1. How many ones are there? Write the number. **2–3.** How many counters are there? Write the number.

**4**

_____

- - - - - - - -

_____

**5**

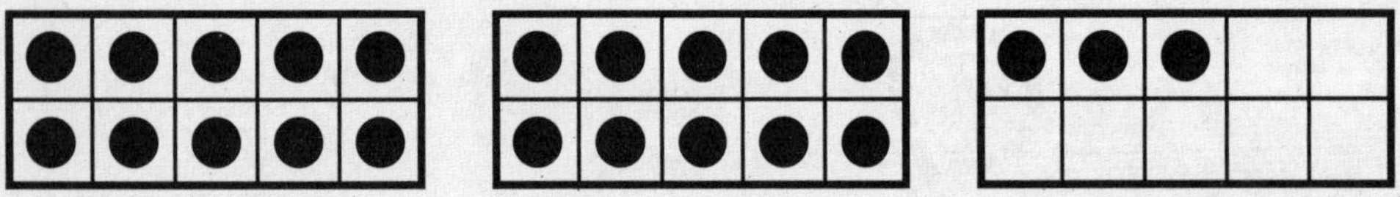

_____

- - - - - - - -

_____

**6**

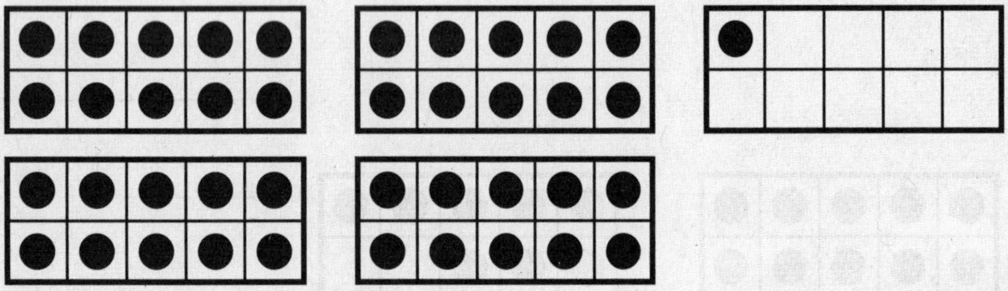

_____

- - - - - - - -

_____

**7**

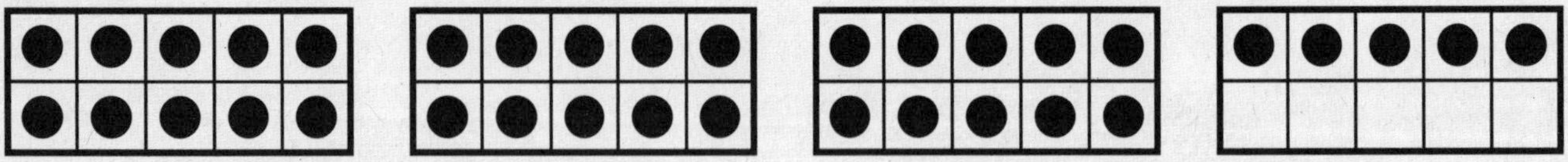

25 ○   30 ○   35 ○   40 ○

**DIRECTIONS 4–6.** How many counters are there? Write the number.
**7.** How many counters are shown? Mark under the number of counters.

Name _____

# Numbers on a Clock

**DIRECTIONS** 1. Trace 12 at the top of the clock. Write the numbers 1 to 6 in order on the clock.

**Getting Ready for Grade 1**

two hundred eighty-nine **P289**

2

1

2

3

4

5

6

---

**DIRECTIONS** **2.** Find 6 on the the clock. Write the numbers 7 to 12 in order on the clock.

**HOME ACTIVITY** • Have your child point to and name the numbers on an analog clock.

**P290** two hundred ninety

# Use an Analog Clock

 o'clock

_____ o'clock

_____ o'clock

_____ o'clock

**DIRECTIONS** **1.** About what time does the clock show?
Trace the number. **2–4.** About what time does the clock show?
Write the number.

before 6 o'clock     about 6 o'clock     after 6 o'clock

**5**

before 2 o'clock

about 2 o'clock

after 2 o'clock

**6**

before 7 o'clock

about 7 o'clock

after 7 o'clock

**7**

before 11 o'clock

about 11 o'clock

after 11 o'clock

**DIRECTIONS** 5–7. Circle the time shown on the clock.

**HOME ACTIVITY** • Look at or draw a simple clock. Ask your child questions such as: *Where does the hour hand go to show about 8 o'clock? About 1 o'clock? About 4 o'clock?*

Name _____

# Use a Digital Clock

 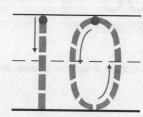 o'clock

_____

- - - - - - -

_____ o'clock

_____

- - - - - - -

_____ o'clock

_____

- - - - - - -

_____ o'clock

**DIRECTIONS   1.** Trace the hour number on the digital clock. Trace to show another way to write that time.   **2–4.** Trace the hour number on the digital clock. Show another way to write that time.

**5**

_____

- - - - - - - - - - -

_____ **o'clock**

 **6**

_____

- - - - - - - - - - -

_____ **o'clock**

**7**

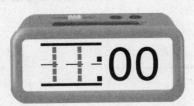

_____

- - - - - - - - - - -

_____ **o'clock**

 **8**

_____

- - - - - - - - - - -

_____ **o'clock**

**DIRECTIONS**  **5–8.** Trace the hour number on the digital clock. Show another way to write that time.

**HOME ACTIVITY** • Ask your child to explain or draw what a digital clock looks like at 3:00.

# ✓ Checkpoint

● ● ● ● ● ● ● ● ● ● ● ● ● ● ● ● ● ● ● ● ● ● ● ● ● ● ● ● ● ● ● ● ● ● ● ● ● ● ● ● ● ● ● ● ● ● ● ● ● ● ●

before 9 o'clock

about 9 o'clock

after 9 o'clock

---

**DIRECTIONS** **1.** Write the missing numbers on the clock. (pp. P289–P290)
**2.** Circle the time shown on the clock. (pp. P291–P292)

**Getting Ready for Grade 1**

**3** 

_____

- - - - - -

_____ **o'clock**

**4** 

**5** 

2        6        7        8

○        ○        ○        ○

**DIRECTIONS**   **3.** Trace the hour number on the clock. Show another way to write that time. **(pp. P293–P294)**   **4.** Write the missing numbers on the clock. **(pp. P289–P290) 5.** Mark under the number that shows about what time is on the clock. **(pp. P291-P292)**

**P296**   two hundred ninety-six